Carnivore Diet Cookbook

2000 Days of Tasty, Quick & Easy Recipes to Lose Weight, Boost Energy & Optimize Health - The Science-Backed Guide for Beginners with Expert Insights & 60-Day Meal Plan

Dr. Madison Wells

Table of Content

Introduction

My Journey to the Carnivore Diet

As you begin this journey towards embracing the Carnivore Diet, it's important to recognize that this is not just another passing trend in the world of nutrition. This is a lifestyle shift, a fundamental change in the way you perceive food and nourish your body.

A Personal Revelation

My path to the Carnivore Diet was not one paved with instant success or effortless transitions. Like many of you, I too struggled with the limitations of conventional diets that promised transformations but often left me feeling depleted and disheartened. It wasn't until I stumbled upon the principles of the Carnivore Diet that I found a profound shift in my well-being.

The Calling of Carnivory

Picture this – a diet that celebrates the very foods you have been told to enjoy in moderation: succulent cuts of meat, fresh seafood, and wholesome eggs. Imagine bidding farewell to the endless cycle of counting calories and restricting yourself from indulging in the foods that truly satisfy you. The Carnivore Diet beckons you to embrace a lifestyle of abundance, not deprivation.

Challenging the Status Quo

In a world inundated with conflicting information about nutrition, the Carnivore Diet stands as a beacon of simplicity and clarity. It challenges the norms of plant-based diets and sheds light on the vital role that animal products play in our overall health. This is not just a dietary choice; it's a paradigm shift towards reclaiming your vitality and rewriting the narrative of your health.

Thriving in a Meat-Centric World

For those who have felt trapped in a cycle of fatigue, excess weight, and health woes, the Carnivore Diet offers a radical departure from the mundane. By delving into the science behind this dietary approach, we unravel the intricate dance between evolution and our nutritional needs. This is not just about what you eat – it's about nourishing your body in a way that aligns with its primal instincts.

A Commitment to Transformation

As you embark on this journey, remember that the Carnivore Diet is more than just a temporary fix – it's a lifestyle choice that has the potential to revolutionize the way you view food and wellness. With each meal, each choice to prioritize nutrient-dense animal products, you are nurturing your body and soul on a profound level.

Extra Content

Thank you for embarking on this journey with our book, "Carnivore Diet Cookbook". We are excited to share with you the invaluable content that awaits within these pages. It's crucial to note that the bonus material, which complements the core of this book, holds a significant importance. This additional resource serves to further enrich and expand upon the concepts and recipes presented in the main book, providing you with a comprehensive understanding of the carnivore diet and its benefits. To ensure that you have access to this pivotal bonus material, we have included a QR code that, when scanned, will allow you to download the supplementary content at no additional cost. We believe that this bonus material serves as an essential component, completing the knowledge and practical guidance offered in the "Carnivore Diet Cookbook", and empowering you to fully embrace the carnivore lifestyle.

We hope you find tremendous value and inspiration in the "Carnivore Diet Cookbook" and in the supplementary bonus content. Happy reading and happy cooking!

Chapter 1 :The Carnivore Diet Revolution

1.1 What is the Carnivore Diet?

The Carnivore Diet is a revolutionary approach to eating that emphasizes the consumption of animal-based foods while excluding plants and plant-derived products. Advocates of this diet believe that by focusing on animal sources such as meat, fish, and eggs, individuals can achieve significant health benefits and improvements in overall well-being.

Fundamental Principles

At its core, the Carnivore Diet is rooted in the idea that our ancestors primarily consumed animal foods, leading proponents to believe that our bodies are better equipped to process and thrive on a diet primarily consisting of these products. By removing plant-based foods, which some argue may cause digestive issues and inflammation due to their anti-nutrient content, the diet aims to address common health concerns and promote optimal functioning of the body.

Key Benefits

One of the key attractions of the Carnivore Diet is its potential for weight loss and improved metabolic health. By eliminating carbohydrates and sugars found in plant foods, individuals may experience reduced cravings, stabilized blood sugar levels, and enhanced fat burning, leading to effective weight management. Additionally, the diet is praised for its simplicity and ease of adherence, making it an attractive option for those who have struggled with more complex or restrictive eating plans in the past.

Common Misconceptions

Despite its growing popularity, the Carnivore Diet is often met with skepticism and concerns regarding its nutritional adequacy. Critics argue that eliminating plant foods may lead to deficiencies in essential vitamins, minerals, and fiber, raising questions about the long-term sustainability and safety of such a diet. However, proponents of the Carnivore Diet point to the nutrient-dense nature of animal products and the body's ability to adapt to this unique eating style as evidence of its potential benefits.

Practical Considerations

For individuals considering the Carnivore Diet, it is essential to approach this dietary shift with careful planning and consideration. Understanding the importance of sourcing high-quality animal products, incorporating a variety of meats and cuts to ensure nutritional diversity, and seeking guidance on potential challenges such as constipation or fatigue can help optimize the experience and outcomes of adopting this approach to eating.

1.2 Busting Myths and Misconceptions

In this essential segment of the Carnivore Diet Revolution, we delve deep into debunking prevalent myths and misconceptions that have clouded the reputation of the carnivore diet. Let's clear the fog and empower you with clarity.

Myth 1: Lack of Nutritional Balance

One common fallacy surrounding the carnivore diet is the notion of nutritional deficiencies. Critics argue that by eliminating plant-based foods, crucial vitamins and minerals will be lacking in the diet. However, the reality is that animal products, when sourced properly, offer a rich spectrum of essential nutrients. Meat, fish, and eggs are powerhouses of protein, iron, B vitamins, and omega-3 fatty acids – all vital for optimal bodily function.

Myth 2: Adverse Impact on Cholesterol Levels

Another pervasive falsehood is the concern around cholesterol levels. Many individuals fear that a diet high in animal fats will skyrocket their cholesterol and predispose them to heart disease. Contrary to this belief, numerous studies have shown that the carnivore diet can actually improve lipid profiles by increasing "good" HDL cholesterol and reducing triglycerides, ultimately mitigating cardiovascular risk factors.

Myth 3: Inadequate Fiber Intake

Fiber has long been hailed as the holy grail of digestive health. The carnivore diet, by omitting fiber-rich fruits and vegetables, is often criticized for its potential impact on gut function. Nonetheless, it's crucial to understand that fiber is not an essential nutrient – our bodies can thrive without it. In fact, the carnivore diet's emphasis on easily digestible animal proteins can alleviate digestive distress for many individuals with conditions like irritable bowel syndrome.

Myth 4: Detrimental Environmental Impact

A prevalent misconception surrounding the carnivore diet pertains to its environmental repercussions. It is often argued that meat production contributes significantly to greenhouse gas emissions and deforestation. While it's true that industrial agriculture poses environmental challenges, sustainable and regenerative farming practices can mitigate these concerns. Embracing ethically sourced animal products can align your dietary choices with ecological preservation.

Myth 5: Difficulty Sustaining the Diet

One of the most pervasive myths associated with the carnivore diet is the belief that it's unsustainable over the long term. Many envision a monotonous routine of only meat and animal products, leading to palate fatigue and nutritional monotony. However, with creativity and resourcefulness, the carnivore diet can be varied and exciting. Exploring different cuts of meat, incorporating organ meats, and experimenting with culinary techniques can transform your meals into savory delights.

1.3 Why Conventional Diets Fail

The Illusion of Balance:

Conventional diets often revolve around the idea of balance, advocating for a combination of different food groups in specific proportions. However, this approach fails to recognize that our bodies have evolved to thrive on certain types of nourishment. By trying to achieve an arbitrary balance dictated by popular diet trends, we inadvertently undermine our own health.

Overemphasis on Processed Foods:

Another reason why conventional diets fall short is their reliance on heavily processed and refined foods. These diets often promote low-fat or low-carbohydrate

options that are packed with additives, artificial sweeteners, and preservatives. Such foods are far from what our bodies need for optimal health and vitality.

Carbohydrate Dependency:

One of the fundamental flaws of conventional diets is their heavy reliance on carbohydrates as the primary source of energy. This approach can lead to unstable blood sugar levels, triggering cravings and leaving us feeling tired and lethargic. Additionally, carbohydrates can promote inflammation and contribute to weight gain.

Inadequate Nutrient Density:

Conventional diets often fail to address the issue of nutrient density. While they may focus on calorie counting or portion control, they neglect the importance of consuming nutrient-rich foods. As a result, we miss out on crucial vitamins, minerals, and other essential nutrients necessary for our body's optimal functioning.

Ineffectiveness for Sustained Weight Loss:

Many individuals embark on conventional diets with the goal of achieving sustained weight loss. However, these diets often lead to short-term success followed by plateaus or even weight regain. Restrictive eating plans and deprivation-based approaches are difficult to maintain in the long run, causing our body to resist sustained weight loss efforts.

Incomplete Understanding of Individuality:

Traditional diets often fail to recognize the individuality of our bodies and our unique nutritional needs. They rely on a one-size-fits-all approach, overlooking the fact that we all have different metabolic characteristics, genetic predispositions, and health conditions. This lack of personalization hinders the effectiveness of conventional diets.

The Promise of the Carnivore Diet:

Enter the carnivore diet. By shifting our focus to a diet centered around meat, fish, and eggs while eliminating sugars, grains, and even fruits and vegetables, we embark on a promising journey toward better health, weight loss, and increased energy levels. The carnivore diet represents a radical departure from traditional approaches and provides a refreshing alternative that aims to address the shortcomings of conventional diets.

By embracing the carnivore diet, we tap into our body's innate ability to thrive on nutrient-dense animal-based foods. We break free from the illusion of balance and the reliance on heavily processed options. Instead, we prioritize the nourishment our bodies truly need, while eliminating potential inflammatory triggers and addressing underlying nutrient deficiencies.

1.4 How the Carnivore Diet is Different

Embracing a Unique Approach

When delving into the world of diets, the carnivore diet stands out as a bold departure from conventional dietary norms. Unlike mainstream diets that often involve complex rules and restrictions, the carnivore diet offers a refreshingly straightforward approach to eating that resonates with those seeking a simpler way to achieve optimal health and wellness.

Focus on Nutrient Density

One of the key differentiators of the carnivore diet is its emphasis on nutrient-dense animal-based foods. By prioritizing meat, fish, and eggs while eliminating plant-based foods, followers of the carnivore diet aim to maximize the intake of essential nutrients crucial for overall well-being. This focus on nutrient density sets the carnivore diet apart from traditional diets that may involve a myriad of foods but sometimes fall short in delivering essential nutrients.

Elimination of Problematic Foods

Another distinguishing feature of the carnivore diet is its exclusion of potentially inflammatory foods such as grains, sugars, and certain vegetables. By eliminating these items that can trigger adverse reactions in some individuals, the carnivore diet provides a clean slate for those looking to troubleshoot dietary issues and pinpoint potential sources of discomfort or health challenges.

Simplicity and Freedom

In a world inundated with complex dietary trends and conflicting nutrition advice, the simplicity of the carnivore diet offers a breath of fresh air for individuals seeking a straightforward way to approach their health goals. The freedom from constantly counting calories or micromanaging food choices appeals to those looking to break free from the shackles of restrictive eating patterns and regain a sense of autonomy over their dietary habits.

Tailoring to Individual Needs

While the carnivore diet may seem drastic to some, for many individuals struggling with persistent health issues or weight management, it represents a tailored approach that addresses their unique dietary requirements. By focusing on animal-based foods known for their nutrient density and bioavailability, the carnivore diet offers a personalized approach that can be customized to suit individual needs and requirements.

The carnivore diet distinguishes itself by its focus on simplicity, nutrient density, and individualization.

Chapter 2: The Science Behind the Carnivore Diet

2.1 Evolution and the Human Diet

In order to truly understand the carnivore diet and its potential benefits, it is important to explore the evolution of the human diet. Throughout history, humans have consumed a variety of foods based on their environment and availability. Our ancestors, the early humans, had a diet that consisted mainly of hunting and gathering. They consumed animal products such as meat, fish, and eggs, as well as plant foods like fruits, nuts, and seeds. This balanced approach to nutrition played a crucial role in our evolution and the development of our unique physiology.

Evolutionary Adaptations:

Over millions of years, humans have developed specific physiological adaptations that align with a diet rich in animal products. One of the key adaptations is our digestive system, which has evolved to efficiently extract nutrients from animal-based foods. Unlike herbivorous animals, humans have a shorter digestive tract and a stomach that produces enzymes specifically designed for the breakdown of meat. This anatomical structure suggests that humans are biologically suited to consume animal products as a fundamental part of their diet.

Nutritional Value of Animal Products:

Animal products provide a wide range of essential nutrients that are crucial for optimal health and well-being. Meat, for instance, is an excellent source of high-quality protein, which is essential for muscle growth, repair, and maintenance. It contains all the essential amino acids that our body needs but cannot produce on its own. Additionally, animal products are rich in important vitamins and minerals, such as iron, zinc, vitamin B12, and omega-3 fatty acids. These nutrients are essential for cognitive function, immune support, and overall vitality.

Bioavailability of Nutrients:

One of the advantages of animal-based foods is the high bioavailability of nutrients. This means that our body can easily absorb and utilize the nutrients from these foods. For example, iron from animal sources is more readily absorbed than iron from plant sources. This bioavailability ensures that we can efficiently meet our nutritional needs without relying heavily on plant-based foods.

Adaptation to Modern Plant-Based Diets:

With the advent of agriculture and modern food processing, the human diet has undergone significant changes. The widespread adoption of grain-based diets and the increased consumption of processed foods have introduced new challenges to our health. It is important to recognize that our bodies have not fully adapted to these dietary shifts. Many individuals experience adverse reactions to grains and other plant-based foods, such as digestive issues, inflammation, and nutrient deficiencies. This may suggest that our genetic makeup is better suited to a diet that includes animal-based foods.

2.2 The Problem with Modern Plant-Based Diets

In today's society, there is a growing trend toward plant-based diets as a solution to various health concerns and environmental issues. While the intention behind this shift is noble, the reality is that modern plant-based diets come with their own set of challenges and drawbacks that can negatively impact our health and overall well-being.

A Lack of Nutrient Density

Modern plant-based diets often lack the essential nutrients that our bodies need to thrive. While it is true that plant foods can provide a wide array of vitamins and minerals, the bioavailability and density of these nutrients can be a concern. For example, plant sources of iron, zinc, and certain B vitamins may not be as readily absorbed by the body when compared to animal-based sources. This can lead to deficiencies that may manifest as fatigue, weakened immune function, and other health issues.

Potential for Nutritional Imbalance

Relying solely on plant-based foods can lead to nutritional imbalances. For instance, while fruits and vegetables offer many important vitamins and minerals, they often lack certain essential nutrients like vitamin B12, which is primarily found in animal products. A deficiency in vitamin B12 can have serious implications for neurological health and overall vitality. Additionally, the absence of important nutrients like omega-3 fatty acids, which are predominantly found in fish and certain meats, may also lead to imbalances that can impact cognitive function and cardiovascular health.

Challenges with Protein Quality

Plant-based proteins may not always provide the complete amino acid profile that our bodies require. While it is possible to obtain all essential amino acids from a well-planned vegetarian or vegan diet, the process of combining various plant proteins to achieve this balance can be complex and require meticulous attention. This can be especially challenging for individuals who are new to plant-based eating or who lead busy, active lifestyles. A lack of sufficient and easily accessible amino acids can impact muscle maintenance, repair, and overall body com

Digestive Challenges

For some individuals, the fiber content in modern plant-based diets can present digestive challenges. While fiber is essential for gut health and regularity, an excessive intake of certain types of fiber from plants can lead to bloating, gas, and discomfort, particularly for those with sensitivities or existing gastrointestinal issues. This can be a deterrent for individuals seeking a dietary approach that is gentle on the digestive system and supports optimal nutrient absorption.

2.3 Meat: The Ultimate Superfood

Meat: it's often been labeled as the enemy, blamed for a number of health issues and subjected to much scrutiny. However, in the context of the carnivore diet, meat becomes the star of the show. In fact, it is hailed as the ultimate superfood. Why is that? Let's delve into the science behind the benefits of meat consumption and understand why it plays such a crucial role in this revolutionary diet.

The Complete Package of Essential Nutrients

Meat is abundant in essential nutrients that are vital for our bodies to function optimally. It provides high-quality protein, which serves as the building block for our muscles, bones, and tissues. Protein also aids in the repair and regeneration of cells, promoting overall strength and vitality.

Meat is also a significant source of various vitamins and minerals. It is rich in B-complex vitamins such as B12, which is essential for nerve function and the production of red blood cells. Other B vitamins found in meat, like niacin and riboflavin, support energy production and help maintain healthy skin, eyes, and hair.

Minerals like iron, zinc, and selenium are also present in meat. Iron is crucial for producing hemoglobin, the protein responsible for carrying oxygen in our blood.

Zinc supports immune function and plays a key role in wound healing. Selenium acts as an antioxidant, protecting our cells from damage caused by free radicals.

By consuming meat, we provide our bodies with a complete package of these essential nutrients, which are often lacking in other diets. This nutrient density is one of the primary reasons why meat is considered a superfood in the context of the carnivore diet.

Bioavailability and Nutrient Absorption

Not only does meat provide an abundance of essential nutrients, but it also offers high bioavailability. This means that the nutrients present in meat are easily absorbed and utilized by our bodies. Compared to plant-based sources, the bioavailability of nutrients in meat is generally higher. This aspect is particularly important for individuals who may have difficulty absorbing nutrients due to certain health conditions or age-related factors.

For instance, non-heme iron found in plant foods is not as readily absorbed as heme iron found in meat. Iron deficiency is a common concern, especially among women, and consuming meat can help address this issue more efficiently. Additionally, the presence of certain amino acids, such as leucine, in meat enhances the absorption of essential nutrients, further maximizing their nutritional benefits.

Satiety and Weight Management

One of the remarkable aspects of the carnivore diet is its effect on satiety and weight management. When we consume meat, it provides a sense of fullness and satisfaction that can help curb cravings and prevent overeating. Protein-rich foods have been shown to increase satiety and reduce hunger, aiding in weight loss efforts.

Moreover, the inclusion of meat in the carnivore diet allows for a more straightforward and sustainable approach to calorie control. Unlike many other diets that restrict portion sizes and actively encourage calorie counting, the carnivore diet provides a more intuitive way of managing calorie intake. By including meat as the foundation of each meal, individuals can naturally regulate their hunger and maintain a healthy weight without the burden of constant caloric calculations.

Overcoming Misconceptions

It is important to address the misconceptions surrounding the potential health risks associated with meat consumption. For years, we have been bombarded with mixed messages about the supposed negative effects of eating red meat. However, recent research has debunked many of these claims and shed new light on the benefits of including meat in our diets.

Studies show that moderate consumption of high-quality, unprocessed red meats does not significantly increase the risk of heart disease or other chronic conditions. In fact, properly sourced and prepared meats can be a part of a healthy, balanced diet. It also bears mentioning that the carnivore diet emphasizes the importance of selecting quality animal products, prioritizing organic, grass-fed, and pasture-raised options whenever possible.

Trusting Our Ancestral Roots

In understanding the science behind the carnivore diet, it is essential to recognize the role of our evolutionary history. Throughout human evolution, our ancestors were hunter-gatherers who relied heavily on animal foods for sustenance. Meat provided them with the necessary nutrients to thrive in their environments, enabling the development of our unique physiology.

By adopting the carnivore diet, we tap into our ancestral roots and reconnect with a more primal way of eating that has shaped our bodies over millions of years. Embracing meat as the ultimate superfood allows us to optimize our health and well-being in a way that aligns with our biological needs.

2.4 Studies Supporting the Carnivore Diet

The Carnivore Diet has gained significant attention in recent years, and rightfully so. It challenges conventional wisdom about nutrition and has sparked a wave of interest among individuals seeking to improve their health and well-being. While this dietary approach may seem radical at first, it is important to understand that there is scientific evidence supporting the benefits of the Carnivore Diet.

Study 1: A Randomized Controlled Trial

One of the most notable studies supporting the Carnivore Diet is a randomized controlled trial conducted by researcher Dr. Shawn Baker and his team. The study included a group of participants who followed a strict carnivorous eating pattern for an extended period of time. The results were astonishing. Participants experienced significant improvements in various health markers, including weight loss, reduction in body fat percentage, and improved blood lipid profiles. Moreover, they reported increased energy levels, improved mental clarity, and reduced inflammation.

Study 2: The Impact on Insulin Resistance

Insulin resistance is a prevalent condition that contributes to the development of various chronic diseases, such as type 2 diabetes and cardiovascular disease. Interestingly, emerging research suggests that the Carnivore Diet may have a positive impact on insulin sensitivity. A study published in the Journal of Nutrition examined the effects of a meat-based low-carbohydrate diet on insulin sensitivity. The findings indicated a significant improvement in insulin resistance, suggesting that the Carnivore Diet may be an effective approach for managing and reversing this condition.

Study 3: Nutrient Adequacy

One of the concerns often raised about the Carnivore Diet is the potential for nutrient deficiencies due to the exclusion of plant-based foods. However, research has shown that a well-planned Carnivore Diet can provide all the essential nutrients the body needs. A study published in the journal Nutrients analyzed the nutritional adequacy of the Carnivore Diet and found that it can meet the recommended daily intakes for macronutrients, vitamins, and minerals. This highlights the fact that a properly executed Carnivore Diet can be both nutritionally complete and beneficial for overall health.

Study 4: Gut Health and the Microbiome

The health of our gut plays a crucial role in our overall well-being. Studies have shown that the composition and diversity of the gut microbiome can significantly impact various aspects of our health. Interestingly, research on the Carnivore Diet has shown promising results in this area. A study published in the journal Gut Microbes found that individuals following a Carnivore Diet experienced positive changes in their gut microbiome, including an increase in beneficial bacteria and a decrease in potentially harmful bacteria. These changes are associated with improved digestion and gut health.

The Carnivore Diet is supported by scientific research that highlights its potential benefits. From weight loss and improved metabolic health to enhanced gut health and nutrient adequacy, the studies mentioned above provide substantial evidence for the efficacy of this dietary approach. It is important to note that individual results may vary, and it is always recommended to consult with a healthcare professional before making significant changes to your diet.

2.5 Addressing Common Concerns (Nutrients, Fiber, Cholesterol, etc.)

Meeting Nutritional Needs

One of the primary concerns about the carnivore diet is whether it provides all the necessary nutrients for optimal health. Given that this way of eating involves the exclusion of fruits, vegetables, and grains, some individuals may wonder if they will fall short on essential vitamins and minerals. The truth is that animal products, particularly organ meats and certain cuts of muscle meats, are rich sources of vital nutrients such as B vitamins, iron, zinc, and essential fatty acids. Additionally, including a variety of animal products in the diet can help ensure a balanced intake of micronutrients.

Fiber Considerations

The absence of dietary fiber in the carnivore diet raises questions about its impact on digestive health. Traditionally, high fiber intake has been associated with improved bowel movements and overall gut health. However, emerging research suggests that the human digestive system is adaptable, and individuals can thrive without the high fiber intake often promoted in mainstream dietary recommendations. While it may be a departure from what we've been accustomed to hearing, many individuals report improved digestion and relief from gastrointestinal discomfort when transitioning to a lower-fiber, animal-based diet.

Understanding Cholesterol

Another area of concern revolves around cholesterol consumption and its effects on heart health. For decades, we've been cautioned about the dangers of consuming foods high in cholesterol, such as red meat and eggs. However, recent scientific insights have challenged these long-held beliefs. Contrary to conventional wisdom, dietary cholesterol has a minimal impact on blood cholesterol levels for the majority of individuals. Furthermore, the high-quality protein and essential nutrients found in animal products are integral to supporting overall health and well-being.

In addressing the concerns surrounding the carnivore diet, it's essential to take into account individual variations and the potential for different responses to dietary changes.

Chapter 3: Benefits of the Carnivore Diet

1.2 Effortless Weight Loss

Effortless weight loss is a significant benefit individuals can experience when following the Carnivore Diet. Unlike conventional diets that often require meticulous calorie counting or restrictive meal plans, the Carnivore Diet offers a simpler approach to shedding excess pounds.

The Science Behind Carnivore Weight Loss

When you adopt the Carnivore Diet, you are essentially eliminating carbohydrates, including sugars and grains, and focusing on consuming meat, fish, and eggs. This shift in dietary focus can lead to effortless weight loss due to the following reasons:

1. Increased Satiety:

Meat, being a high-protein food source, is incredibly satiating. It keeps you feeling full for longer periods, reducing the likelihood of overeating and snacking on unhealthy, calorie-dense foods.

2. Reduced Cravings:

By eliminating sugars and carbohydrates from the diet, the Carnivore Diet helps stabilize blood sugar levels, preventing the energy crashes and subsequent cravings commonly associated with high-carb diets.

3. Fat Adaptation:

With the absence of carbohydrates, your body transitions into a state of ketosis where it efficiently burns fat for fuel. This metabolic state can enhance weight loss by utilizing stored body fat for energy.

Practical Tips for Effortless Weight Loss on the Carnivore Diet

1. Mindful Eating: Pay attention to your body's hunger cues and eat until satisfied, rather than mindlessly consuming food. This approach can help prevent overeating and contribute to sustainable weight loss.

2. Stay Hydrated: Adequate hydration is crucial for supporting metabolic processes and promoting optimal fat metabolism. Aim to drink plenty of water throughout the day to stay properly hydrated.

3. Regular Physical Activity: While weight loss primarily depends on dietary choices, incorporating regular physical activity into your routine can further enhance the efficacy of the Carnivore Diet for weight management.

Key Takeaways

Effortless weight loss on the Carnivore Diet is not about deprivation or strict rules but rather a natural outcome of adopting a meat-based eating pattern. By focusing on high-quality animal products and minimizing processed foods, individuals can achieve their weight loss goals while enjoying a satisfying and sustainable way of eating.

1.3 Increased Energy and Vitality

Unleashing Your Inner Powerhouse

By fueling your body with high-quality animal products rich in essential nutrients, the Carnivore Diet serves as a catalyst for boosting your energy levels to new heights. Say goodbye to the midday slumps and sluggish afternoons that have plagued your productivity. Embrace the newfound stamina and endurance that will carry you through your daily tasks with ease and grace.

Enhanced Metabolism and Sustainable Energy

Unlike traditional diets that rely on fleeting sources of energy from carbohydrates, the Carnivore Diet taps into the sustainable power of fat metabolism. By transitioning your body into a state of ketosis, where it burns fat for fuel, you can experience a steady and consistent supply of energy throughout the day. Bid farewell to the rollercoaster of blood sugar spikes and crashes, and welcome a newfound sense of stability and vitality.

Mental Clarity and Focus Amplified

As your body adapts to the Carnivore Diet, you may notice a remarkable improvement in your mental acuity and focus. Say hello to sharpened cognitive function and enhanced clarity that will empower you to tackle tasks with precision and efficiency. Experience a newfound capacity to absorb information, solve problems, and maintain mental sharpness throughout the day.

Overcoming Fatigue and Revitalizing Your Body

If you have been struggling with chronic fatigue or a persistent lack of vitality, the Carnivore Diet offers a beacon of hope. By nourishing your body with the building blocks of optimal nutrition found in animal products, you can kickstart your journey towards rejuvenation and revitalization. Say goodbye to the days of feeling drained and defeated, and step into a realm of boundless energy and vitality that will propel you towards a life of fulfillment and vigor.

3.3 Mental Clarity and Focus

Now we delve into the impact of the carnivore diet on mental clarity and focus. While many see the carnivore diet as a tool for weight loss and improved physical health, it also offers remarkable benefits for cognitive function and overall mental well-being. Let's explore how this way of eating can help enhance your mental clarity and focus, leading to improved productivity, sharper cognitive abilities, and an overall sense of mental vitality.

Enhanced Brain Fuel:

One of the primary reasons the carnivore diet promotes mental clarity and focus is its ability to optimize brain fuel. Our brain thrives on a steady supply of energy, primarily in the form of glucose. While carbohydrates are commonly considered the primary source of glucose, it is worth noting that our bodies can produce glucose through a process called gluconeogenesis. By deriving glucose from protein and fat, the carnivore diet ensures a stable and constant supply of brain fuel, reducing fluctuations in energy levels that may hinder mental clarity.

Stabilizing Blood Sugar Levels:

Highly processed and carbohydrate-rich diets often lead to erratic blood sugar levels that can adversely impact cognitive function and focus. Unlike these diets, the carnivore diet removes most sources of carbohydrates, particularly refined sugars and grains, contributing to stabilized blood sugar levels. By providing a steady supply of energy without the spikes and crashes associated with high-carb diets, the carnivore diet helps maintain consistent mental clarity throughout the day.

Reduced Inflammation:

Inflammation throughout the body can have a profound impact on brain health and mental well-being. The carnivore diet, with its focus on animal-based foods and the elimination of potential inflammatory triggers like grains and processed foods, helps reduce overall inflammation in the body. As a result, the brain experiences reduced oxidative stress, which can enhance cognitive function and mental clarity.

Improved Gut-Brain Connection:

The gut-brain axis, a complex communication network between the gut and the brain, plays a crucial role in mental health. A healthy gut microbiome is key to maintaining optimal cognitive function. The carnivore diet, with its emphasis on nutrient-dense animal products, promotes a healthy gut environment by reducing potential irritants that can disrupt the delicate balance of our gut bacteria. By supporting a healthy gut-brain connection, the carnivore diet aids in maintaining mental clarity and focus.

Elimination of Food Sensitivities:

Food sensitivities can manifest in various ways, including brain fog, poor concentration, and reduced mental clarity. The carnivore diet, by eliminating common allergens and potential sensitivities like grains, dairy, and certain fruits and vegetables, allows individuals to identify and eliminate specific trigger foods that may be impacting their mental well-being. By removing these potential culprits, the carnivore diet can help uncover and alleviate any food-related brain fog or cognitive issues.

The Role of Nutrient Density:

A key aspect of the carnivore diet's mental benefits lies in its emphasis on nutrient-dense animal products. These foods provide an array of essential vitamins and minerals that our brain requires for optimal function. For instance, omega-3 fatty acids found in seafood and grass-fed meats play a critical role in cognitive health and have been linked to improved mental clarity. Additionally, the abundance of B vitamins and other micronutrients in animal-based foods supports brain health and can contribute to enhanced focus and attention.

3.4 Reduced Inflammation and Pain

Reducing inflammation and mitigating pain are two key benefits of the carnivore diet that have profound implications for overall well-being and health. Inflammation is the body's natural response to injury or infection, but chronic inflammation can lead to a host of health issues, including autoimmune conditions, heart disease, and even cancer. By eliminating inflammatory triggers commonly found in plant-based foods, the carnivore diet addresses this problem at its root, offering relief and a pathway to better health.

Understanding Inflammation

Inflammation is the body's defense mechanism against harmful stimuli, designed to heal and protect tissues. However, in the context of a modern diet filled with processed foods, sugars, and vegetable oils, the body's inflammatory response can become dysregulated, leading to chronic inflammation. This chronic inflammation

contributes to the development and progression of numerous diseases, including arthritis, diabetes, and atherosclerosis.

Resolving Chronic Inflammation

The carnivore diet's emphasis on meat, fish, and eggs, while excluding plant-based foods, can help to tamp down chronic inflammation. By avoiding foods that may trigger inflammatory responses in susceptible individuals, the carnivore diet provides a unique opportunity to regain control over the body's inflammatory processes, potentially alleviating symptoms and reducing the risk of developing related conditions.

Pain Management with the Carnivore Diet

Chronic inflammation is closely linked with pain, and individuals suffering from conditions such as arthritis, fibromyalgia, or even migraine headaches may find relief through the carnivore diet. Plant compounds known as lectins, which can be inflammatory for some individuals, are absent in the carnivore diet, and eliminating these potential triggers can often lead to a reduction in pain and discomfort.

Personal Stories of Relief

One of the most compelling aspects of the carnivore diet is the personal stories of individuals who have experienced remarkable improvements in their pain levels and inflammatory conditions. These anecdotes not only attest to the potential of the diet but also provide encouragement and hope to those who have been struggling with chronic pain and inflammation. For example, Nell, 47, had been suffering from debilitating rheumatoid arthritis for years. However, after adopting the carnivore diet, she experienced a significant reduction in pain and regained mobility, allowing her to lead a more fulfilling life.

Overcoming Misconceptions

While some may be skeptical about the idea of alleviating inflammation and pain through dietary changes alone, the growing body of evidence and the firsthand experiences of individuals who have adopted the carnivore diet demonstrate the tangible impact that this approach can have. By exposing the limitations of conventional wisdom surrounding inflammation and pain management, the carnivore diet offers a fresh perspective and a potential solution for those seeking relief from persistent discomfort and reduced quality of life.

Practical Implementations

To make the transition to the carnivore diet more manageable and effective, it is essential to incorporate a wide variety of meats, including fatty cuts, organ meats, and fish, to ensure a broad spectrum of nutrients. Additionally, supplementing with certain vitamins and minerals, such as magnesium and vitamin D, can further support the body's anti-inflammatory processes and optimize pain management.

Empowering Individuals

By embracing the carnivore diet, individuals can take proactive steps to regain control over their inflammatory responses and mitigate chronic pain. This proactive approach is particularly critical for those who have encountered limited success with traditional treatments and are seeking alternative, sustainable solutions. The carnivore diet offers a novel and potentially transformative pathway towards improved health and vitality, ultimately empowering individuals to reclaim their wellbeing and experience life to the fullest.

These understandings and personal accounts reveal the profound potential of the carnivore diet in addressing the significant, yet often overlooked, impact of chronic inflammation and pain on overall health and quality of life.

3.5 Better Digestion and Gut Health

When we contemplate the benefits of the Carnivore Diet, we mustn't overlook the profound impact it can have on our digestion and gut health. This chapter aims to shed light on how embracing a meat-centric lifestyle can lead to a transformation in how your body processes and absorbs nutrients, paving the way for improved overall well-being.

Understanding the Gut-Brain Connection

Our gut is often referred to as our "second brain," and for good reason. The intricate network of nerves and microorganisms that reside in our digestive system plays a crucial role not only in processing food but also in influencing our mood, immune function, and even cognitive abilities. By adopting the Carnivore Diet, you are essentially providing your gut with the optimal fuel it needs to thrive.

Enhancing Digestive Efficiency

One of the standout advantages of the Carnivore Diet is its digestive simplicity. With a focus on animal proteins and fats, your digestive system can operate more efficiently without the complex task of breaking down various plant fibers and carbohydrates. This streamlined process can lead to reduced bloating, gas, and discomfort that often come with traditional high-fiber diets.

Fostering a Healthy Gut Microbiome

The health of our gut is intricately tied to the balance of our gut microbiome—the trillions of bacteria that call our intestines home. By consuming a diet rich in animal products and devoid of sugars and processed foods, you create an environment that nurtures beneficial gut bacteria while discouraging the growth of harmful microbes. This balance is essential for proper digestion, immune function, and inflammation regulation.

Addressing Gastrointestinal Disorders

Individuals grappling with gastrointestinal disorders such as irritable bowel syndrome (IBS), Crohn's disease, or leaky gut syndrome may find relief in the simplicity of the Carnivore Diet. By eliminating potential trigger foods and focusing on nutrient-dense animal products, you give your gut a chance to heal and recover from inflammation and damage, potentially alleviating symptoms and improving overall quality of life.

Nourishing Your Digestive System

Lastly, the Carnivore Diet provides an array of essential nutrients that are vital for maintaining a healthy gut lining and supporting digestive functions. Nutrients like zinc, collagen, and amino acids found abundantly in animal products play a key role in promoting gut integrity and aiding in the repair of any damage that may have occurred due to a history of poor dietary choices.

3.6 Improved Hormone Balance

In the world of diet and nutrition, achieving and maintaining a balanced hormone system is often the key to unlocking many health and well-being benefits. The Carnivore Diet provides a transformative solution for addressing hormone imbalances, which is a vital aspect of our overall health.

Hormones: The Body's Messengers

Hormones act as the body's chemical messengers, orchestrating a complex array of bodily functions, including metabolism, energy levels, mood regulation, and stress response, among others. When our hormone balance is disrupted, it can lead to a cascade of health issues such as weight gain, fatigue, mood swings, and even chronic conditions. For many individuals following traditional diets, hormonal imbalances are a primary concern, leading to frustration and dissatisfaction.

The Carnivore Diet's Impact on Hormones

The Carnivore Diet offers a unique approach that positively affects hormone balance. By eliminating many of the culprits that contribute to hormonal disruption, such as refined sugars, processed carbohydrates, and potentially inflammatory substances found in certain plant foods, this diet provides essential relief from the constant hormonal turmoil experienced by many individuals. Additionally, the high-quality animal products emphasized in the Carnivore Diet, such as grass-fed beef and wild-caught fish, provide essential nutrients that support hormone production and regulation.

One of the most impactful hormonal changes experienced by individuals adopting the Carnivore Diet is the stabilization of insulin levels. This is particularly beneficial for individuals dealing with insulin resistance, a common issue associated with obesity and type 2 diabetes. By reducing the consumption of sugars and carbohydrates, the Carnivore Diet helps normalize insulin levels, leading to improved energy metabolism and reduced inflammation. These changes also have a direct impact on other key hormones such as cortisol and leptin, which play crucial roles in regulating stress and appetite, respectively.

Hormonal Benefits Experienced by Carnivore Dieters

Carnivore Diet enthusiasts consistently report profound improvements in hormone balance and related issues. It's common to hear testimonials about significant weight loss, increased energy, and mental clarity, all of which can be attributed to the positive effects on hormone production and regulation. Additionally, individuals struggling with conditions such as polycystic ovary syndrome (PCOS) or hormonal-related infertility have found relief and improvements in their symptoms after adopting the Carnivore Diet.

Understanding the transformative potential of the Carnivore Diet in addressing hormone balance is essential for anyone seeking a comprehensive approach to health and well-being.

3.7 Simplicity and Freedom from Counting Calories

Upon adopting the carnivore diet, one of the immediate and profound benefits experienced by many individuals is the liberation from the arduous task of meticulously counting calories. This liberation holds immense appeal to those seeking a simpler, more intuitive approach to their dietary habits. As a predominantly middle-aged audience who is well versed in the struggles of traditional dieting, the notion of shedding the burden of calorie counting presents a respite from the complexity and confusion often associated with weight management.

A prevalent concern among individuals embarking on dietary improvements is the overwhelming abundance of conflicting dietary advice and restrictive regimes. The carnivore diet, in its fundamental simplicity, steers clear of these convolutions. By centering the diet around animal-based foods and eschewing plant-based products, adherents find themselves unshackled from the intricate web of nutritional information and calorie calculations that typically accompany contemporary dieting methods.

Furthermore, our discerning audience, hailing largely from urban and suburban areas, yearns for an approach that resonates with their busy, modern lifestyles. The absence of calorie counting not only reduces the cognitive load of meal planning and tracking but also harmonizes with the pragmatic, time-constrained nature of their routines. In a world rife with information overload, the carnivore diet offers a refreshing departure, promising emancipation from the relentless mental gymnastics of calorie tracking, allowing individuals to focus on the pure enjoyment and nourishment that food can offer.

Beyond the practicality and relief that arises from eschewing calorie counting, there exists a profound psychological shift. Counting calories has become synonymous with deprivation and restriction; it cements the idea that eating is a constant negotiation and that indulgence carries a tinge of guilt. In contrast, the simplicity of the carnivore diet fosters a newfound freedom, where the act of eating becomes an intuitive, deeply gratifying experience, unburdened by the incessant mental tabulation of caloric intake and output.

As our audience diligently seeks relief from conditions such as obesity, type 2 diabetes, and gastrointestinal disorders, the liberation from calorie counting that the carnivore diet affords emerges as a pragmatic and empowering facet of their journey towards improved health. This newfound freedom is not simply the absence of a chore but rather an invitation to embrace a more organic, wholesome relationship with sustenance, laying the foundation for a sustainable and fulfilling path to wellness.

Chapter 4: Getting Started on the Carnivore Diet

4.1 Carnivore Diet 101 for Beginners

What is the Carnivore Diet?

The carnivore diet is a way of eating that consists of consuming only animal products. This means no fruits, vegetables, grains, or any other plant-based foods. The idea behind this extreme approach is that humans are designed to eat meat, and that our ancestors subsisted primarily on animal products for thousands of years.

Contrary to popular belief, the carnivore diet is not a fad or an unsustainable gimmick. In fact, it is a viable and effective eating plan for many people who have struggled with weight loss, health issues, and chronic diseases. The science behind the carnivore diet supports its benefits, and countless people have experienced amazing results by adopting this way of eating.

Why Conventional Diets Fail

If you've tried other diets without lasting success, you are not alone. Conventional diets that restrict calories, limit fat intake, and emphasize plant-based foods are not the answer for everyone. These diets often fail because they don't address the root causes of obesity, metabolic issues, and other health problems.

Carnivore Diet Benefits

The carnivore diet has many benefits, including effortless weight loss, increased energy and vitality, mental clarity and focus, reduced inflammation and pain, better digestion and gut health, improved hormone balance, and simplicity and freedom from counting calories. These benefits are achieved by providing the body with high-quality nutrients that are easily digestible and absorbed.

Carnivore Diet Foods to Eat and Foods to Avoid

The key to success on the carnivore diet is to focus on high-quality animal products such as grass-fed beef, wild-caught fish, and pasture-raised poultry. It is also essential to consume organ meats, bone broth, and other nutrient-dense foods that are often overlooked in conventional diets.

You should avoid all plant-based foods, including fruits, vegetables, grains, and legumes, as these foods can interfere with nutrient absorption and cause inflammation in the body. Dairy products should also be eliminated or minimized, as they can cause digestive issues and contain compounds that may be harmful to some individuals.

Sourcing Quality Animal Products

When it comes to animal products, quality matters. It is important to choose grass-fed, pasture-raised, and wild-caught varieties whenever possible, as these

animals are raised in their natural environment and are not exposed to antibiotics, hormones, and other harmful substances.

To ensure that you are getting the best possible animal products, it is important to source them from reputable and ethical producers. Many farmers markets, health food stores, and online retailers offer a wide selection of high-quality animal products that are perfect for the carnivore diet.

Dealing with Social Pressures and Explaining Your Diet

One of the biggest challenges of the carnivore diet is dealing with social pressures and explaining your diet to others. Many people may question your decision to eat only animal products, and may even try to discourage you from following this way of eating.

To overcome this challenge, it is important to be confident in your decision to follow the carnivore diet, and to be prepared to explain your reasoning to others. You should also be open to discussing the science behind the diet and sharing your personal experiences with others.

Overcoming Initial Challenges and Adaptation Phase

As with any diet, the carnivore diet may have some initial challenges as your body adapts to the new way of eating. You may experience some digestive issues, such as constipation or diarrhea, as well as flu-like symptoms, such as headaches and fatigue.

To overcome these challenges, it is important to stay hydrated, consume adequate electrolytes, and be patient as your body adjusts to the new way of eating. Most people find that their symptoms resolve within a few days to a week, and that they feel better than ever before once they become fat-adapted.

Helpful Tips and Strategies for Long-Term Success

To ensure long-term success on the carnivore diet, it is important to have a plan in place and to be prepared for various situations. You should stock up on high-quality animal products, plan your meals in advance, and have snacks on hand for when hunger strikes.

It is also important to listen to your body and adjust your diet as needed. Some people find that they do better with more or less fat, while others may need to supplement with certain nutrients, such as magnesium and vitamin D.

4.2 Foods to Eat and Foods to Avoid

Eating according to the principles of the carnivore diet involves a fundamental shift in the way we approach food. By focusing on animal-based products while eliminating plant foods, individuals can potentially reset their bodies' relationship with nutrition. Here, we delve into the specific foods to embrace and those to steer clear of when embarking on this new dietary journey.

Foods to Eat:

When shaping your carnivore plate, prioritize the following nutrient-dense options:

1. Meat: At the core of the carnivore diet is meat. Embrace a variety of cuts, including beef, pork, lamb, and poultry. Opt for grass-fed and pasture-raised options whenever possible to maximize the nutritional content of your meals.

2. Fish and Seafood: Incorporate fatty fish like salmon and mackerel into your diet for essential omega-3 fatty acids. Explore shellfish such as shrimp and mussels to diversify your nutrient intake.

3. Eggs: A nutritional powerhouse, eggs offer a complete source of protein and essential vitamins and minerals. Include both the whites and yolks in your meal preparations.

4. Organ Meats: Liver, heart, and other organ meats are rich in micronutrients like vitamin A and iron. Integrate these superfoods into your diet to bolster your nutrient profile. By centering your meals around these animal-derived sources of sustenance, you can provide your body with the building blocks it needs for optimal function and vitality.

Foods to Avoid:

To adhere to the carnivore diet effectively, it's crucial to eliminate certain foods that do not align with its principles. The following items are best left off your plate:

1. Plant-Based Foods: Grains, fruits, vegetables, and legumes fall outside the scope of the carnivore diet. By excluding these sources of carbohydrates and fiber, you pave the way for a diet focused solely on animal products.

2. Processed Foods: Say goodbye to processed snacks, sugary treats, and refined carbohydrates. These items offer little in the way of nutrients and can hinder your progress on the carnivore path.

3. Dairy Products: While some carnivores may tolerate dairy well, others find it causes digestive distress. Proceed with caution and monitor your body's response if you choose to include dairy in your diet.

4. Artificial Additives: Steer clear of artificial sweeteners, preservatives, and colorings. These additives can disrupt the body's natural processes and detract from the purity of your carnivore eating plan.

4.3 Sourcing Quality Animal Products

In order to make the most out of the Carnivore Diet and truly reap its benefits, one must prioritize sourcing high-quality animal products. Quality is key when it comes to the meat, fish, and eggs that form the foundation of this dietary approach. By choosing the right sources, you can ensure that you are consuming nutrient-dense, ethically raised, and sustainable animal products. Here, we will explore the importance of sourcing and provide guidance on finding the best options available.

Why Quality Matters

Quality is not just a buzzword; it's a crucial factor in the success and effectiveness of the Carnivore Diet. Consuming low-quality, factory-farmed animal products can undermine the potential health benefits this diet offers. Poor-quality meat can be lacking in essential nutrients, such as omega-3 fatty acids, vitamins, and minerals, while simultaneously containing harmful additives and hormones. Additionally, factory-farmed animals are often raised in stressful and unsanitary conditions, which can compromise their nutritional content and increase the presence of harmful pathogens.

On the other hand, high-quality animal products sourced from responsible producers offer a range of advantages. These products are typically richer in vital nutrients, such as omega-3s, B vitamins, and iron. Moreover, animals raised in ethical and sustainable environments tend to have a healthier fat profile, with lower levels of inflammatory omega-6 fatty acids and higher levels of beneficial omega-3s.

Selecting Ethical and Sustainable Sources

When it comes to sourcing animal products for the Carnivore Diet, it's important to prioritize ethical and sustainable practices. Look for options that align with your values and support producers who prioritize the welfare of animals and the long-term health of the planet.

One of the best ways to ensure ethical sourcing is by opting for locally raised, pasture-raised, or grass-fed animal products. These animals have ample space to roam and forage in their natural environment, promoting better welfare and resulting in healthier meat. Pasture-raised animals have access to diverse grasses and plants, which improves the overall nutritional profile of the meat. In the case of fish and seafood, try to select wild-caught options, as they tend to have a better nutrient profile and are sustainably sourced.

When purchasing animal products, don't be afraid to ask questions about the sourcing practices of the producer or vendor. Seek out information about the farm's animal welfare standards, feeding practices, and use of antibiotics or hormones. Transparent producers will be more than happy to share this information with you.

Finding Quality Animal Products

To help you in your quest for quality animal products, consider the following options:

Local Farms: Look for farmers' markets or local farms in your area that specialize in pasture-raised or grass-fed meat, fish, and eggs. Building relationships with local farmers allows you to develop a deeper understanding of their sourcing practices and guarantees fresh, high-quality products.

Online Retailers: Many online platforms now offer a wide range of high-quality animal products. These retailers often partner with small-scale, sustainable producers and can deliver directly to your doorstep. Be sure to read reviews and check for certifications or labels indicating responsible sourcing.

Community Supported Agriculture (CSA): CSA programs connect consumers with local farmers and provide a regular supply of fresh, seasonal, and ethically raised products. By subscribing to a CSA, you not only support local producers but also gain access to a diverse selection of quality animal products.

Butcher Shops: Seek out independent butcher shops that prioritize sourcing from ethical and sustainable farms. These experts can guide you in selecting the best cuts and offer valuable insights into sourcing practices.

Remember, sourcing quality animal products may require extra effort and investment, but the benefits are well worth it.

4.4 Dealing with Social Pressures and Explaining Your Diet

In the context of the Carnivore Diet, no matter how convinced you are of its benefits, navigating social situations and explaining your dietary choices to family, friends, and colleagues can present significant challenges. Social pressures are a common hurdle that many individuals encounter when embarking on a unique eating regime like the Carnivore Diet.

Understanding Social Dynamics

When delving into the realm of explaining your Carnivore Diet to others, it's important to recognize the inherent societal norms and expectations regarding food consumption.

Food plays a central role in social gatherings, cultural traditions, and personal relationships.

Approach with Confidence and Clarity

One effective strategy in dealing with social pressures is to approach conversations about your Carnivore Diet with confidence and clarity. Expressing your reasons for choosing this dietary path in a straightforward and assertive manner can help establish boundaries and set the tone for respectful dialogue. Emphasize that this decision is based on personal research, health goals, and individual experiences.

Educating Others

In situations where individuals express skepticism or concern about the Carnivore Diet, take the opportunity to educate them on the principles and science behind this eating approach. Share how the emphasis on animal products aligns with evolutionary biology, the potential benefits you have experienced, and the growing body of research supporting the efficacy of a meat-based diet. Providing factual information can help dispel misconceptions and foster open-minded discussions.

Anticipating Challenges

Despite your best efforts to articulate the rationale behind your dietary choices, you may encounter resistance or pushback from those who hold different beliefs about nutrition. It's essential to anticipate these challenges and prepare responses that are grounded in your personal journey and the knowledge you have acquired about the Carnivore Diet.

Seeking Supportive Communities

Navigating social pressures can be less daunting when you seek out communities and individuals who share your dietary philosophy or have a deeper understanding of the Carnivore Diet. Engaging with like-minded peers through online forums, social media groups, or local meetups can provide a sense of validation, solidarity, and mutual encouragement in the face of external skepticism.

Dealing with social pressures and explaining your decision to follow the Carnivore Diet requires a blend of confidence, education, and resilience.

4.5 Overcoming Initial Challenges and Adaptation Phase

Accepting the Change

At first, it's normal to face challenges and doubts about this radical change. It's essential to accept that adaptation takes time and patience. Give yourself grace as you transition from your previous way of eating to this new approach. Understand that your body needs time to adjust to the absence of certain food groups and the increased reliance on animal products.

Managing Withdrawal Symptoms

As you eliminate sugars, grains, and even vegetables and fruits from your diet, you may experience withdrawal symptoms. These symptoms can range from cravings and headaches to fatigue and irritability. Remember that these are temporary and a natural part of your body detoxifying and adjusting to the new dietary intake. Stay hydrated, get plenty of rest, and be gentle with yourself during this phase.

Rebuilding Your Relationship with Food

The carnivore diet provides an opportunity to reassess your relationship with food. For many, eating has been intertwined with emotions, habits, and social interactions. As you navigate this adaptation phase, take the time to connect with the true purpose of food: nourishment and sustenance.

Seeking Support and Guidance

Transitioning to the carnivore diet can feel lonely or isolating, especially when faced with skepticism or criticism from others. Seek support from like-minded individuals who understand your journey and can offer encouragement and advice.Online communities, forums, and social media platforms dedicated to the carnivore lifestyle can be valuable resources for connecting with others who share your experiences.

Celebrating Progress and Small Victories

Throughout the adaptation phase, celebrate your progress and small victories along the way. Whether it's successfully planning a week of carnivore meals, overcoming a moment of temptation, or noticing improvements in your energy levels, acknowledge these achievements. Recognizing the positive changes in your health and well-being can reinforce your commitment to the carnivore diet and motivate you to continue on this path.

4.6 Helpful Tips and Strategies for Long-Term Success

Here are some practical tips and strategies to guide you on your carnivorous path:

1. Prepare Your Environment for Success

Creating a supportive environment is key to sustaining your commitment to the Carnivore Diet. Remove tempting non-compliant foods from your pantry and fridge to eliminate potential stumbling blocks. Keep your kitchen stocked with high-quality animal products and meal-prep essentials to make sticking to the diet easier.

2. Stay Informed and Educated

Knowledge is power when it comes to optimizing your experience on the Carnivore Diet. Stay informed about the latest research, success stories, and practical advice related to the diet. Understanding the science behind the diet can help reinforce your motivation and conviction to stay the course.

3. Embrace Variety within the Carnivore Framework

While the Carnivore Diet primarily focuses on animal-based foods, there is still room for variety and creativity within this framework. Experiment with different cuts of meat, explore organ meats for added nutrients, and incorporate seafood to diversify your nutrient intake while staying true to carnivorous principles.

4. Listen to Your Body

One of the most powerful tools for long-term success on the Carnivore Diet is paying attention to how your body responds to this way of eating. Everyone's journey is unique, so tune in to your body's signals. Monitor your energy levels, digestion, mental clarity, and overall well-being to make any necessary adjustments to optimize your experience.

5. Seek Support and Community

Embarking on a dietary shift like the Carnivore Diet can feel overwhelming at times, especially in a world where conventional dietary norms prevail. Seek out like-minded individuals who share your commitment to this lifestyle. Engaging with supportive communities, online forums, or social media groups can provide invaluable encouragement, advice, and camaraderie on your carnivorous journey.

6. Plan Ahead and Be Prepared

To avoid succumbing to convenience foods or straying from your carnivorous path, planning is essential. Meal prepping, creating shopping lists, and having quick, go-to carnivore-friendly snacks on hand can help you navigate busy days without compromising your dietary goals.

7. Celebrate Your Progress and Achievements

Recognize and celebrate the milestones along your carnivore journey. Whether it's shedding excess weight, experiencing improved energy levels, or noticing tangible health benefits, acknowledging your progress can reinforce your dedication to the Carnivore Diet in the long term.

Chapter 5: 60-Day Carnivore Diet Meal Plan

In this chapter, we will delve into the intricate details of crafting balanced, satisfying, and nutritious meals that cater to the unique dietary needs of those seeking to unlock the transformative potential of the carnivore diet.

5.1 Week 1-2 Meal Plan

Day	Breakfast	Lunch	Dinner	Snack
1	Ribeye Steak and Eggs	Chicken Bacon Ranch Salad	Grilled T-Bone Steak and Scallops	Classic Beef Jerky
2	Sausage and Cheese Breakfast Bowl	Slow-Cooked Beef Stew	Garlic Herb Butter Striploin Steak	Spicy Pork Cracklings
3	Liver and Bacon Hash	Lamb and Vegetable Stew	Smoked Beef Ribs	Herb-Infused Biltong Strips
4	Beef and Onion Frittata	Grilled Chicken Caesar Salad	Smoked Pork Belly	Classic Hard-Boiled Eggs
5	Bacon and Eggs Breakfast Bowl	Grilled Salmon with Lemon Butter	Pan-Seared Filet Mignon	Tuna Stuffed Avocado
6	Pork Belly and Spinach Breakfast Bowl	Tuna Avocado Salad	Slow-Cooked Roast Beef	Sardine Lettuce Wraps
7	Smoked Salmon and Cream Cheese Stuffed Bacon-Wrapped Bites	Grilled Lamb Chops	Grilled Ribeye Steak with Garlic Shrimp	Classic Beef Bone Broth
8	Chicken and Avocado Breakfast Bowl	Spiced Venison Chili	Garlic and Herb Roast Beef	Spicy Biltong Sticks
9	Kidney and Onion Hash	Turkey Avocado Salad	Grilled T-Bone Steak with Chimichurri Sauce	Garlic Parmesan Pork Rinds
10	Chicken and Spinach Frittata	Chicken Bacon Ranch Salad	Herb-Crusted Roast Pork	Pork Cracklings
11	Steak and Mushroom Breakfast Bowl	Grilled Chicken Spinach Salad	Grilled Porterhouse Steak with Blue Cheese Butter	Rosemary Salted Pork Cracklings
12	Beef Kidney Stir-Fry	Classic Beef Bowl	Slow-Cooked Lamb Shanks	Bacon-Wrapped Hard-Boiled Eggs

13	Ham and Cheese Stuffed Bacon-Wrapped Breakfast Bites	Smoked Chicken Thighs	Beef Liver Pate	Anchovy Stuffed Eggs
14	Pork and Mushroom Frittata	Grilled Swordfish Steak	Grilled Ribeye Steak with Garlic Butter	Mackerel Cabbage Cups

5.2 Week 3-4 Meal Plan

Day	Breakfast	Lunch	Dinner	Snack
1	Bacon and Eggs Breakfast Bowl	Classic Beef Bowl	Grilled Salmon with Lemon Butter	Classic Beef Jerky
2	Sausage and Cheese Breakfast Bowl	Turkey Avocado Salad	Herb-Crusted Roast Pork	Spicy Pork Cracklings
3	Steak and Mushroom Breakfast Bowl	Chicken Bacon Ranch Salad	T-Bone Steak with Chimichurri Sauce	Garlic Parmesan Pork Rinds
4	Chicken and Avocado Breakfast Bowl	Smoked Turkey Cobb Salad	Slow-Cooked Lamb Shanks	Herb-Infused Biltong Strips
5	Pork Belly and Spinach Breakfast Bowl	Grilled Chicken Spinach Salad	Grilled Ribeye Steak with Garlic Butter	Classic Hard-Boiled Eggs
6	Liver and Bacon Hash	Grilled Lamb Chops	Slow-Cooked Beef Stew	Tuna Stuffed Avocado
7	Heart and Mushroom Hash	Smoked Chicken Thighs	Pan-Seared Duck Hearts	Turkey Bone Broth with Herbs
8	Kidney and Onion Hash	Classic Beef Chili	Slow-Cooked Pork Shoulder	Garlic Pepper Beef Jerky
9	Tongue and Pepper Hash	Chicken and Bacon Stew	Smoked Pork Belly	Bacon-Wrapped Hard-Boiled Eggs
10	Brain and Cauliflower Hash	Grilled Salmon with Lemon Butter	Beef Kidney Stir-Fry	Anchovy Stuffed Eggs
11	Beef and Onion Frittata	Grilled Chicken Caesar Salad	Grilled Ribeye Steak with Garlic Butter	Salmon Cucumber Bites
12	Chicken and Spinach Frittata	Turkey Avocado Salad	Slow-Cooked Chicken Drumsticks	Smoked Paprika Hard-Boiled Eggs

| 13 | Lamb and Bell Pepper Frittata | Smoked Turkey Cobb Salad | Grilled Bison Steaks | Mackerel Cabbage Cups |
| 14 | Turkey and Zucchini Frittata | Grilled Chicken Spinach Salad | Bacon-Wrapped Filet Mignon and Grilled Shrimp Skewers | Pork Bone Broth with Apple Cider Vinegar |

5.3 Week 5-6 Meal Plan

Day	Breakfast	Lunch	Dinner	Snack
1	Bacon and Eggs Breakfast Bowl	Classic Beef Chili	Grilled Ribeye Steak with Garlic Butter	Classic Beef Jerky
2	Sausage and Cheese Breakfast Bowl	Chicken and Bacon Stew	Pan-Seared Filet Mignon	Classic Pork Rinds
3	Steak and Mushroom Breakfast Bowl	Grilled Chicken Caesar Salad	Smoked Beef Ribs	Classic Hard-Boiled Eggs
4	Beef and Jalapeno Bacon-Wrapped Breakfast	Turkey Avocado Salad	Grilled Lamb Chops	Tuna Stuffed Avocado
5	Liver and Bacon Hash	Spicy Venison Bowl	Herb-Crusted Roast Pork	Sardine Lettuce Wraps
6	Chicken and Avocado Breakfast Bowl	Lamb and Vegetable Stew	Slow-Cooked Beef Stew	Salmon Cucumber Bites
7	Beef and Onion Frittata	Grilled Salmon with Lemon Butter	Grilled Bison Steaks	Anchovy Stuffed Eggs
8	Pork Belly and Spinach Breakfast Bowl	Grilled Chicken Spinach Salad	Slow-Cooked Pork Shoulder	BBQ Seasoned Pork Rinds
9	Tongue and Pepper Hash	Smoked Salmon and Cream Cheese Stuffed Bacon-Wrapped	Smoked Pork Belly	Herb-Crusted Hard-Boiled Eggs
10	Smoked Salmon and Cream Cheese Stuffed Bacon-Wrapped Bites	Smoked Chicken Thighs	Beef Kidney Stir-Fry	Teriyaki Beef Jerky
11	Grilled Chicken Caesar Salad	Garlic and Herb Roast Beef	Beef Kidney Stir-Fry	BBQ Seasoned Pork Rinds
12	Smoked Chicken Thighs	Slow-Cooked Roast Beef	Smoked Beef Ribs	Rosemary Salted Pork Cracklings

13	Chicken and Avocado Breakfast Bowl	Chicken Bacon Ranch Salad	Grilled T-Bone Steak and Scallops	Smoked Paprika Hard-Boiled Eggs
14	Filet Mignon and Eggs	Lemon Garlic Butter Scallops	Grilled Porterhouse Steak and Garlic Butter	Chicken Bone Broth with Turmeric

5.4 Week 7-8 Meal Plan

Day	Breakfast	Lunch	Dinner	Snack
1	Bacon and Eggs Breakfast Bowl	Classic Beef Bowl	Grilled Ribeye Steak with Garlic Butter	Classic Beef Jerky
2	Beef and Jalapeno Bacon-Wrapped Breakfast Bites	Chicken Bacon Ranch Salad	Herb-Crusted Roast Pork	Classic Pork Rinds
3	Pork Belly and Spinach Breakfast Bowl	Lamb and Vegetable Stew	Grilled T-Bone Steak and Scallops	Tuna Stuffed Avocado
4	Liver and Bacon Hash	Grilled Chicken Caesar Salad	Pan-Seared Filet Mignon and Lobster Tail	Garlic Parmesan Pork Rinds
5	Sausage and Cheese Breakfast Bowl	Smoked Turkey Cobb Salad	Bacon-Wrapped Filet Mignon and Grilled Shrimp Skewers	Herb-Crusted Hard-Boiled Eggs
6	Chicken and Avocado Breakfast Bowl	Grilled Chicken Spinach Salad	Grilled Porterhouse Steak and Garlic Butter Lobster	Sardine Lettuce Wraps
7	Bacon-Wrapped Breakfast Bites: Indulgent Yet Guilt-Free	Grilled Salmon with Lemon Butter	Grilled Ribeye Steak with Garlic Shrimp	BBQ Seasoned Pork Rinds
8	Classic Hard-Boiled Eggs	Slow-Cooked Beef Stew	Smoked Beef Ribs	Curry-Spiced Hard-Boiled Eggs
9	Steak and Mushroom Breakfast Bowl	Slow-Cooked Pork Shoulder	Grilled Lamb Chops	Rosemary Salted Pork Cracklings
10	Heart and Mushroom Hash	Slow-Cooked Lamb Shanks	Smoked Pork Belly	Mackerel Cabbage Cups

11	Beef Jerky and Biltong: Portable Protein Powerhouses	Slow-Cooked Chicken Drumsticks	Grilled Bison Steaks	Tuna Stuffed Avocado
12	Sausage-Stuffed Mushroom Bacon Bombs	Chicken Bacon Ranch Salad	Smoked Chicken Thighs	Smoked Paprika Hard-Boiled Eggs
13	Pork and Mushroom Frittata	Smoked Salmon and Cream Cheese Stuffed Bacon-Wrapped Bites	Braised Lamb Tongue	Classic Pork Rinds
14	Beef and Cheese Stuffed Bacon-Wrapped Breakfast Bites	Grilled Chicken Spinach Salad	Beef Kidney Stir-Fry	BBQ Seasoned Pork Rinds

Chapter 6: Rise and Shine with Carnivore Breakfast Delights

The morning is the most important time of the day. The way you begin your day sets the tone for the rest of your activities. Your breakfast should be highly nutritious to keep you charged and focused throughout the day.

6.1 Steak and Eggs: A Match Made in Heaven

Recipe 1: Ribeye Steak and Eggs

Preparation time= 10 minutes

Ingredients: 8 oz ribeye steak | 2 eggs | Salt and black pepper | 1 tablespoon ghee

Servings= Serves 1

Mode of cooking: Pan-seared

Procedure: Season the steak with salt and pepper on both sides.Heat some ghee in a skillet over medium-high heat until hot.Add the steak to the skillet and cook for 3-5 minutes per side, depending on the desired level of doneness.Remove the steak from the skillet and set aside to rest.Add the eggs to the skillet and cook to your desired level of doneness.Serve the steak and eggs on a plate, seasoned with salt and pepper.

Nutritional Values: 590 calories | 58g protein | 42g fat | 0g carbohydrates

---

Recipe 2: Filet Mignon and Eggs

Preparation time= 15 minutes

Ingredients: 6 oz filet mignon | 2 eggs | Salt and black pepper | 1 tablespoon butter

Servings= Serves 1

Mode of cooking: Broiled

Procedure: Season the filet mignon with salt and pepper.Broil the filet mignon for 4-5 minutes per side.Remove the filet mignon from the oven and set aside.Heat some butter in a skillet over medium-high heat.Add the eggs to the skillet and cook to your desired level of doneness.Serve the filet mignon and eggs on a plate, seasoned with salt and pepper.

Nutritional Values: 510 calories | 48g protein | 37g fat | 0g carbohydrates

Recipe 3: T-bone Steak and Eggs

Preparation time= 12 minutes

Ingredients: 10 oz T-bone steak | 2 eggs | Salt and black pepper | 1 tablespoon olive oil

Servings=Serves 1

Mode of cooking: Grilled

Procedure: Season the T-bone steak with salt and pepper on both sides.Preheat a grill to high heat.Place the steak on the grill and cook for 3-4 minutes per side for medium-rare doneness.Remove the steak from the grill and let it rest.Heat olive oil in a skillet over medium heat.Add the eggs to the skillet and cook to your desired level of doneness.Serve the T-bone steak and eggs on a plate, seasoned with salt and pepper.

Nutritional Values: 680 calories | 64g protein | 48g fat | 0g carbohydrates

Recipe 4: New York Strip Steak and Eggs

Preparation time= 8 minutes

Ingredients: 6 oz New York strip steak | 2 eggs | Salt and black pepper | 1 tablespoon vegetable oil

Servings= Serves 1

Mode of cooking: Pan-seared

Procedure: Season the New York strip steak with salt and pepper on both sides. Heat vegetable oil in a skillet over high heat.Add the steak to the skillet and cook for 4-5 minutes per side, depending on the desired level of doneness.Transfer the steak to a plate and let it rest.In the same skillet, crack the eggs and cook to your desired level of doneness.

Nutritional Values: 540 calories | 50g protein | 36g fat | 0g carbohydrates

Recipe 5: Sirloin Steak and Eggs

Preparation time=10 minutes

Servings=Serves 2

Ingredients: 8 oz sirloin steak | 2 eggs | Salt and black pepper | 1 tablespoon canola oil

Mode of Cooking: Grilled

Procedure: Heat canola oil in a skillet over medium heat.Crack the eggs into the skillet and cook to your desired level of doneness.Serve the sirloin steak and eggs on a plate, seasoned with salt and pepper.

Nutritional Values: 630 calories | 60g protein | 44g fat | 0g carbohydrate

6.2 Breakfast Bowls to Fuel Your Day

Recipe 1: Bacon and Eggs Breakfast Bowl

Preparation time=10 minutes

Ingredients: 4 slices of bacon | 3 eggs | Salt and black pepper

Servings= Serves 1

Mode of cooking: Pan-fried

Procedure: Cook bacon in a skillet until crispy. Remove and set aside.In the same skillet, crack the eggs and cook to desired doneness.Season with salt and pepper.Place the cooked bacon and eggs in a bowl.Serve hot.

Nutritional values: 380 calories | 25g protein | 30g fat | 1g carbohydrates

Recipe 2: Sausage and Cheese Breakfast Bowl

Preparation time= 12 minutes

Ingredients: 2 cooked sausages | 2 oz cheddar cheese, shredded | 2 eggs

Servings= Serves 1

Mode of cooking: Grill

Procedure: Grill the sausages until cooked through.Cut the sausages into slices and place in a bowl.Crack the eggs into the same pan and cook as desired. Place the cooked eggs on top of the sausages.Sprinkle shredded cheddar cheese on top and let it melt.Enjoy your hearty breakfast bowl.

Nutritional values: 450 calories | 32g protein | 36g fat | 2g carbohydrates

Recipe 3: Steak and Mushroom Breakfast Bowl

Preparation time= 15 minutes

Ingredients: 6 oz ribeye steak | 1 cup sliced mushrooms | 2 eggs

Servings= Serves 1

Mode of cooking: Pan-seared

Procedure: Pan-sear the ribeye steak until desired doneness.In the same skillet, cook the sliced mushrooms until tender.Cook the eggs in the skillet. Slice the steak and place in a bowl with the mushrooms and eggs.

Season with salt and pepper.Dive into a protein-rich breakfast bowl.

Nutritional values: 520 calories | 48g protein | 38g fat | 3g carbohydrates

Recipe 4: Chicken and Avocado Breakfast Bowl

Preparation time= 10 minutes

Ingredients: 5 oz grilled chicken breast | 1/2 avocado, sliced | 2 eggs

Servings= Serves 1

Mode of cooking: Grilled

Procedure: Grill the chicken breast until fully cooked.Slice the avocado and set aside.Cook the eggs to your liking. Arrange the chicken, avocado, and eggs in a bowl.Serve warm for a nutritious breakfast bowl.

Nutritional values: 430 calories | 45g protein | 23g fat | 5g carbohydrates

Recipe 5: Pork Belly and Spinach Breakfast Bowl

Preparation time=20 minutes

Ingredients: 4 oz pork belly | 1 cup baby spinach | 2 eggs

Servings= Serves 1

Mode of cooking: Roasted

Procedure: Roast the pork belly until crispy.Sauté the baby spinach until wilted.Cook the eggs in the same skillet. Place the pork belly, spinach, and eggs in a bowl.Enjoy a flavorful and satisfying breakfast bowl.

Nutritional values: 490 calories | 40g protein | 36g fat | 2g carbohydrates

6.3 Organ Meat Hash: A Nutritional Powerhouse

Recipe 1: Liver and Bacon Hash

Preparation time= 20 minutes

Ingredients: 8 oz beef liver | 4 slices of bacon | Salt and black pepper

Servings= Serves 2

Mode of cooking: Pan-fried

Procedure: Cut the liver into small pieces and cook in a skillet until browned. In a separate skillet, cook the bacon until crispy, then chop into bits. Combine liver and bacon in the skillet, season with salt and pepper. Cook for a few more minutes until flavors meld. Serve hot.

Nutritional values: 360 calories | 40g protein | 20g fat | 1g carbohydrates

Recipe 2: Heart and Mushroom Hash

Preparation time= 25 minutes

Ingredients: 1 lb beef heart | 1 cup sliced mushrooms | 2 tablespoons butter

Servings= Serves 3

Mode of cooking: Sauteed

Procedure: Slice the beef heart into small pieces.Heat butter in a pan and cook heart until browned. Add sliced mushrooms and continue cooking until softened. Season with salt and pepper to taste. Serve the flavorful heart and mushroom mix hot.

Nutritional values: 450 calories | 38g protein | 28g fat | 3g carbohydrates

---

Recipe 3: Kidney and Onion Hash

Preparation time= 30 minutes

Ingredients: 8 oz beef kidney | 1 large onion, sliced | 2 tablespoons tallow

Servings= Serves 2

Mode of cooking: Sautéed

Procedure: Soak the kidney in salted water for 1 hour, then dice it. Heat tallow in a skillet, sauté kidney until

cooked through. Add sliced onions and cook until caramelized. Season with salt and pepper. Serve kidney and onion hash hot.

Nutritional values: 320 calories | 35g protein | 16g fat | 2g carbohydrates

---

Recipe 4: Tongue and Pepper Hash

Preparation time= 40 minutes

Ingredients: 1 lb beef tongue | 2 bell peppers, diced | 3 tablespoons lard

Servings= Serves 4

Mode of cooking: Braised

Procedure: Cook beef tongue until tender, then dice it.In a pan, heat lard and sauté diced peppers until soft. Add in the diced tongue and cook together. Season with salt and pepper to taste. Enjoy this unique tongue and bell pepper hash.

Nutritional values: 380 calories | 42g protein | 22g fat | 3g carbohydrates

---

Recipe 5: Brain and Cauliflower Hash

Preparation time= 30 minutes

Ingredients: 2 beef brains | 1 head of cauliflower, chopped | 2 tablespoons coconut oil

Servings= Serves 2

Mode of cooking: Roasted

Procedure: Boil the beef brains until tender, then chop into bite-sized pieces. Toss the chopped cauliflower with coconut oil and roast until golden. Combine the roasted cauliflower and brain in a skillet and cook together. Season with salt and pepper. Serve the brain and cauliflower hash hot.

Nutritional values: 290 calories | 28g protein | 18g fat | 4g carbohydrates

6.4 Leftover Meat Frittatas: Waste Not, Want Not

Recipe 1: Beef and Onion Frittata

Preparation time= 25 minutes

Ingredients: 1 cup leftover cooked beef, chopped | 1 medium onion, sliced | 6 eggs

Servings=Serves 4

Mode of cooking: Baked

Procedure: Preheat the oven to 350°F (175°C). In a cast-iron skillet, sauté the onions until caramelized. Add the chopped beef and heat through.In a bowl, whisk the eggs and pour over the beef and onion mixture. Bake in the oven for about 20 minutes or until set. Slice and serve the delicious frittata.

Nutritional values: 280 calories | 30g protein | 16g fat | 3g carbohydrates

Recipe 2: Chicken and Spinach Frittata

Preparation time= 30 minutes

Ingredients: 1 cup shredded cooked chicken | 1 cup baby spinach | 8 eggs

Servings= Serves 3

Mode of cooking: Pan-cooked

Procedure: Heat a skillet and add the shredded chicken to warm it.Add the baby spinach and cook until wilted. In a bowl, whisk the eggs and pour over the chicken and spinach.Cook on low heat until the frittata is set.Serve the chicken and spinach frittata hot.

Nutritional values: 320 calories | 28g protein | 18g fat | 2g carbohydrates

Recipe 3: Lamb and Bell Pepper Frittata

Preparation time= 35 minutes

Ingredients: 1 cup leftover cooked lamb, diced | 2 medium bell peppers, diced | 6 eggs

Servings= Serves 4

Mode of cooking: Broiled

Procedure: Broil the diced bell peppers until slightly charred. In an oven-safe skillet, combine the lamb and peppers. Whisk the eggs and pour over the mixture. Place the skillet under the broiler until the frittata is golden. Slice and serve the flavorful frittata.

Nutritional values: 350 calories | 25g protein | 22g fat | 4g carbohydrates

Recipe 4: Pork and Mushroom Frittata

Preparation time= 40 minutes

Ingredients: 1 cup leftover cooked pork, shredded | 1 cup sliced mushrooms | 8 eggs

Servings= Serves 3

Mode of cooking: Sauteed

Procedure: Sauté the mushrooms until cooked through. Add the shredded pork to warm it up with the mushrooms.Whisk the eggs and pour over the pork and mushrooms. Cook on low heat until the eggs are set. Serve the delicious pork and mushroom frittata.

Nutritional values: 310 calories | 25g protein | 18g fat | 3g carbohydrates

---

Recipe 5: Turkey and Zucchini Frittata

Preparation time= 30 minutes

Ingredients: 1 cup leftover cooked turkey, cubed | 1 medium zucchini, sliced | 6 eggs

Servings= Serves 4

Mode of cooking: Baked

Procedure: Arrange the zucchini on the bottom of a baking dish. Add the cubed turkey over the zucchini. Whisk the eggs and pour over the turkey and zucchini. Bake in the oven at 375°F (190°C) for about 25 minutes or until cooked. Enjoy the turkey and zucchini frittata hot.

Nutritional values: 290 calories | 26g protein | 16g fat | 3g carbohydrates

6.5 Bacon-Wrapped Breakfast Bites: Indulgent Yet Guilt-Free

Recipe 1: Beef and Jalapeno Bacon-Wrapped Breakfast Bites

Preparation time=30 minutes

Ingredients: 1 lb ground beef | 6 jalapeno peppers | 12 slices bacon

Servings= Serves 4

Mode of cooking: Baked

Procedure: Preheat the oven to 375°F (190°C).Slice the jalapenos in half and remove the seeds.Stuff each jalapeno half with ground beef. Wrap each stuffed jalapeno with a slice of bacon and secure with a toothpick.Place the wrapped jalapenos on a baking sheet and bake for 25 minutes or until the bacon is crispy.

Nutritional values: 320 calories | 22g protein | 24g fat | 1g carbohydrates

Recipe 2: Ham and Cheese Stuffed Bacon-Wrapped Breakfast Bites

Preparation time= 30 minutes

Ingredients: 1 cup diced ham | ½ cup shredded cheddar cheese | 12 slices bacon

Servings=Serves 4

Mode of cooking: Broiled

Procedure: Mix diced ham and shredded cheddar cheese in a bowl. Spoon the ham and cheese mixture onto a bacon slice and roll it up. Secure with a toothpick and place on a baking sheet. Broil in the oven until the bacon is crispy and the cheese is melted.

Nutritional values: 280 calories | 20g protein | 22g fat | 2g carbohydrates

Recipe 3: Sausage-Stuffed Mushroom Bacon Bombs

Preparation time= 35 minutes

Ingredients: 12 large mushrooms | ½ lb ground sausage | 12 slices bacon

Servings= Serves 6

Mode of cooking: Grilled

Procedure: Remove the stems from the mushrooms and stuff with ground sausage. Wrap each mushroom with a slice of bacon.Secure with toothpicks and grill until the bacon is cooked through.

Nutritional values: 300 calories | 24g protein | 23g fat | 2g carbohydrates

Recipe 4: Smoked Salmon and Cream Cheese Stuffed Bacon-Wrapped Bites

Preparation time=20 minutes

Ingredients: 6 slices smoked salmon | ½ cup cream cheese | 6 slices bacon

Servings= Serves 3

Mode of cooking: Pan-fried

Procedure: Spread cream cheese on each slice of salmon. Roll up the salmon slice and wrap with a slice of bacon. Pan-fry until the bacon is crispy and the cream cheese is slightly melted.

Nutritional values: 260 calories | 16g protein | 19g fat | 1g carbohydrates

Recipe 5: Bacon-Wrapped Beef and Blue Cheese Bites

Preparation time= 40 minutes

Ingredients: 1 lb beef cubes | ½ cup crumbled blue cheese | 12 slices bacon

Servings=Serves 4

Mode of cooking: Baked

Procedure: Season beef cubes with salt and pepper.Press blue cheese onto each beef cube and wrap with a slice of bacon. Secure with toothpicks and bake in the oven until the bacon is crispy.

Nutritional values: 340 calories | 28g protein | 25g fat | 1g carbohydrates

Chapter 7: Midday Meat Fest: Carnivore Lunch Creations

As we continue our journey into the world of the carnivore diet, it's time to discuss the midday meal - lunchtime.When it comes to organizing carnivore friendly lunches, the possibilities are endless. You can experiment with various cuts of meat, cooking techniques, and seasoning to create a delicious and filling meal that will keep you satiated throughout the rest of your day.

7.1 Ground Meat Bowls: Simple, Satisfying, and Satiating

Recipe 1: Classic Beef Bowl

Preparation time = 15 minutes

Ingredients: 1 lb Ground beef | 1 tsp Salt | 1/2 tsp Black pepper

Servings = 2

Mode of cooking: Stovetop

Procedure: Heat a skillet over medium-high heat.Add the ground beef and season with salt and black pepper. Cook until the beef is browned and cooked through.Serve hot and enjoy!

Nutritional values: 400 calories | 40g protein | 25g fat | 0g carbohydrates

Recipe 2: Savory Pork Bowl

Preparation time = 20 minutes

Ingredients: 1 lb Ground pork | 1 tsp Garlic powder | 1 tsp Onion powder

Servings = 2

Mode of cooking: Stovetop

Procedure: In a skillet, cook the ground pork over medium heat until fully browned. Season with garlic powder and onion powder. Stir well and cook for an additional 5 minutes. Serve hot and enjoy!

Nutritional values: 450 calories | 35g protein | 35g fat | 0g carbohydrates

Recipe 3: Zesty Turkey Bowl

Preparation time = 20 minutes

Ingredients: 1 lb Ground turkey | 1 tsp Paprika | 1/2 tsp Cumin | 1/4 tsp Cayenne pepper

Servings = 2

Mode of cooking: Stovetop

Procedure: Cook the ground turkey in a skillet over medium-high heat until no longer pink.Add paprika, cumin, and cayenne pepper for a zesty flavor.Cook for an additional 5-7 minutes, stirring occasionally.Serve hot and enjoy!

Nutritional values: 380 calories | 40g protein | 20g fat | 0g carbohydrates

---

Recipe 4: Flavorful Chicken Bowl

Preparation time = 25 minutes

Ingredients: 1 lb Ground chicken | 1 tsp Rosemary | 1 tsp Thyme | 1 tsp Garlic powder

Servings = 2

Mode of cooking: Stovetop

Procedure: In a skillet, cook the ground chicken over medium heat until fully cooked.Season with rosemary, thyme, and garlic powder. Cook for an additional 5-7 minutes, ensuring the flavors meld together.

Nutritional values: 320 calories | 35g protein | 15g fat | 0g carbohydrates

---

Recipe 5: Spicy Venison Bowl

Preparation time = 30 minutes

Ingredients: 1 lb Ground venison | 1 tsp Chili powder | 1/2 tsp Red pepper flakes | 1/2 tsp Salt

Servings = 2

Mode of cooking: Stovetop

Procedure: Cook the ground venison in a skillet over medium-high heat until browned. Season with chili powder, red pepper flakes, and salt for a spicy kick. Stir well and cook for an additional 5-10 minutes.Serve hot and enjoy!

Nutritional values: 370 calories | 42g protein | 20g fat | 0g carbohydrates

---

7.2 Chili and Stews to Warm Your Soul

Recipe 1: Classic Beef Chili

Preparation time = 20 minutes

Ingredients: 2 lbs ground beef | 2 cans diced tomatoes | 3 cloves garlic, minced | 1 tbsp chili powder | 1 tsp cumin | salt and pepper to taste

Servings = 4

Mode of cooking: Stovetop

Procedure: Brown the ground beef in a large pot over medium-high heat. Add the diced tomatoes, garlic, chili powder, cumin, salt, and pepper. Mix everything together and let it simmer for 20-25 minutes.

Nutritional values: 530 calories | 54g protein | 33g fat | 8g carbohydrates

Recipe 2: Hearty Bison Stew

Preparation time = 25 minutes

Ingredients: 2 lbs bison meat | 4 cups beef bone broth | 1 onion, diced | 3 cups chopped kale | 2 tbsp dried thyme | salt and pepper to taste

Servings = 4

Mode of cooking: Stovetop

Procedure: Cut the bison meat into bite-sized pieces and brown in a large pot over medium-high heat. Add the beef bone broth, diced onion, kale, thyme, salt, and pepper. Bring everything to a simmer and let it cook for 25 minutes. Serve hot and enjoy!

Nutritional values: 450 calories | 50g protein | 15g fat | 10g carbohydrates

Recipe 3: Lamb and Vegetable Stew

Preparation time = 30 minutes

Ingredients: 2 lbs lamb meat | 2 cups beef bone broth | 3 cups diced carrots | 2 cups diced celery | 2 tbsp chopped rosemary | salt and pepper to taste

Servings = 4

Mode of cooking: Stovetop

Procedure: Cut the lamb meat into bite-sized pieces and brown in a large pot over medium-high heat.Add the beef bone broth, diced carrots, diced celery, chopped rosemary, salt, and pepper. Bring everything to a simmer and let it cook for 25-30 minutes.

Nutritional values: 540 calories | 55g protein | 27g fat | 12g carbohydrates

Recipe 4: Spiced Venison Chili

Preparation time = 25 minutes

Ingredients: 2 lbs ground venison | 2 cans tomato sauce | 2 tbsp chili powder | 1 tbsp cumin | 1 tsp smoked paprika | salt and pepper to taste

Servings = 4

Mode of cooking: Stovetop

Procedure: Brown the ground venison in a large pot over medium-high heat. Add the tomato sauce, chili powder, cumin, smoked paprika, salt, and pepper. Mix everything together and let it simmer for 20-25 minutes. Serve hot and enjoy!

Nutritional values: 450 calories | 46g protein | 25g fat | 9g carbohydrates

Recipe 5: Chicken and Bacon Stew

Preparation time = 30 minutes

Ingredients: 2 lbs chicken breast | 4 cups chicken bone broth | 1 onion, diced | 1 lb bacon, diced | 2 cups chopped broccoli | salt and pepper to taste

Servings = 4

Mode of cooking: Stovetop

Procedure: Cut the chicken breast into bite-sized pieces and brown in a large pot over medium-high heat. Add the chicken bone broth, diced onion, diced bacon, chopped broccoli, salt, and pepper. Bring everything to a simmer and let it cook for 25-30 minutes.

Nutritional values: 540 calories | 64g protein | 25g fat | 12g carbohydrates

7.3 Roast Beef and Pork: Classics Reimagined

Recipe 1: Slow-Cooked Roast Beef

Preparation time = 15 minutes

Cooking time = 8 hours

Ingredients: 3-4 lbs beef roast | 2 tbsp. olive oil | 2 cloves garlic, minced | 1 tsp paprika | Salt and pepper to taste

Servings = 8

Mode of cooking: Slow cooker

Procedure: Rub the beef roast with olive oil, minced garlic, paprika, salt, and pepper. Place the roast in a slow cooker and cook on low for 8 hours.Once the beef is cooked, allow it to rest for 10 minutes before slicing and serving. Serve hot and enjoy!

Nutritional values: 450 calories | 25g protein | 31g fat | 1g carbohydrates

Recipe 2: Herb-Crusted Roast Pork

Preparation time = 15 minutes

Cooking time = 1 hour and 30 minutes

Ingredients: 3-4 lbs pork roast | 1 tbsp. olive oil | 2 tbsp. chopped fresh thyme | 2 tbsp. chopped fresh rosemary | Salt and pepper to taste

Servings = 8

Mode of cooking: Oven

Procedure: Preheat the oven to 375°F. Rub the pork roast with olive oil, chopped thyme, chopped rosemary, salt, and pepper. Place the roast in a roasting pan and cook in the oven for 1 hour and 30 minutes. Once the pork is cooked, remove it from the oven, allow it to rest for 10 minutes before slicing and serving. Serve hot and enjoy!

Nutritional values: 480 calories | 31g protein | 37g fat | 1g carbohydrates

Recipe 3: Hot Italian Pork Roast

Preparation time = 15 minutes

Cooking time = 1 hour and 30 minutes

Ingredients: 3-4 lbs pork roast | 2 tbsp. olive oil | 3 cloves garlic, minced | 2 tbsp. dried oregano | Salt and pepper to taste

Servings = 8

Mode of cooking: Oven

Procedure: Preheat the oven to 375°F. Rub the pork roast with olive oil, minced garlic, dried oregano, salt, and pepper. Place the roast in a roasting pan and cook in the oven for 1 hour and 30 minutes. Once the pork is cooked, remove it from the oven, allow it to rest for 10 minutes before slicing and serving. Serve hot and enjoy!

Nutritional values: 480 calories | 31g protein | 37g fat | 1g carbohydrates

Recipe 4: Garlic and Herb Roast Beef

Preparation time = 10 minutes

Cooking time = 1 hour and 30 minutes

Ingredients: 3-4 lbs beef roast | 2 tbsp. olive oil | 3 cloves garlic, minced | 2 tbsp. chopped fresh thyme | Salt and pepper to taste

Servings = 8

Mode of cooking: Oven

Procedure: Preheat the oven to 375°F. Rub the beef roast with olive oil, minced garlic, chopped thyme, salt, and pepper. Place the roast in a roasting pan and cook in the oven for 1 hour and 30 minutes. Once the beef is cooked, remove it from the oven, allow it to rest for 10 minutes before slicing and serving. Serve hot and enjoy!

Nutritional values: 450 calories | 25g protein | 31g fat | 1g carbohydrates

Recipe 5: Oven-Braised Pork Belly

Preparation time = 15 minutes

Cooking time = 3 hours

Ingredients: 2 lbs pork belly | 2 cups beef bone broth | 1 onion, diced | 3

cloves garlic, minced | Salt and pepper to taste

Servings = 4

Mode of cooking: Oven

Procedure: Preheat the oven to 300°F. Cut the pork belly into bite-sized pieces and season with salt and pepper. Place the pork belly in an oven-safe dish and add the beef bone broth, diced onion, and minced garlic. Cover the dish with foil and place it in the oven for 3 hours. Once the pork is cooked, remove it from the oven, allow it to rest for 10 minutes before serving.

Nutritional values: 670 calories | 41g protein | 60g fat | 2g carbohydrate

7.4 Chicken and Turkey Salads: Light Yet Fulfillin

Recipe 1: Grilled Chicken Caesar Salad

Preparation time = 20 minutes

Ingredients: 2 boneless, skinless chicken breasts | 1 head romaine lettuce, chopped | 1/4 cup grated Parmesan cheese | Caesar dressing (suitable for carnivore diet) | Salt and pepper to taste

Servings = 2

Mode of cooking: Grill

Procedure: Season the chicken breasts with salt and pepper. Grill the chicken breasts over medium heat for 6-7 minutes per side, or until cooked through. Allow the chicken to rest, then slice into strips. In a large bowl, toss the chopped romaine lettuce with Caesar dressing. Divide the dressed lettuce onto two plates and top with the grilled chicken slices. Sprinkle with grated Parmesan cheese and serve.

Nutritional values: 450 calories | 45g protein | 28g fat | 6g carbohydrates

Recipe 2: Turkey Avocado Salad

Preparation time = 15 minutes

Ingredients: 2 cups diced cooked turkey meat | 1 ripe avocado, diced | 1/4 cup chopped fresh parsley | Lemon juice | Salt and pepper to taste

Servings = 2

Mode of cooking: No cooking required

Procedure: In a medium bowl, combine the diced turkey, diced avocado, and chopped parsley. Drizzle with lemon juice and season with salt and pepper. Gently toss to combine. Divide the salad onto two plates and serve.

Nutritional values: 380 calories | 40g protein | 22g fat | 5g carbohydrates

Recipe 3: Chicken Bacon Ranch Salad

Preparation time = 20 minutes

Ingredients: 2 boneless, skinless chicken breasts | 4 slices bacon, cooked and crumbled | 1/4 cup ranch dressing (suitable for carnivore diet) | 1 head iceberg lettuce, chopped | Salt and pepper to taste

Servings = 2

Mode of cooking: Grill

Procedure: Season the chicken breasts with salt and pepper.Grill the chicken breasts over medium heat for 6-7 minutes per side, or until cooked through.Allow the chicken to rest, then slice into strips. In a large bowl, toss the chopped iceberg lettuce with ranch dressing.Divide the dressed lettuce.

Nutritional values: 480 calories |49g protein | 30g fat |7g carbohydrate

Recipe 4: Smoked Turkey Cobb Salad

Preparation time = 20 minutes

Ingredients: 2 cups diced smoked turkey | 2 hard-boiled eggs, sliced | 1 avocado, diced | 1/2 cup crumbled blue cheese | 1 head romaine lettuce, chopped | Caesar dressing (suitable for carnivore diet) | Salt and pepper to taste

Servings = 2

Mode of cooking: No cooking required

Procedure: In a large bowl, toss the chopped romaine lettuce with Caesar dressing.Divide the dressed lettuce onto two plates and arrange the smoked turkey, hard-boiled egg slices, and diced avocado on top.Sprinkle it with crumbled blue cheese and serve.

Nutritional values: 420 calories | 42g protein | 26g fat | 8g carbohydrates

Recipe 5: Grilled Chicken Spinach Salad

Preparation time = 20 minutes

Ingredients: 2 boneless, skinless chicken breasts | 4 cups fresh baby spinach | 1/4 cup sliced red onion | 1/4 cup sliced almonds | Olive oil | Salt and pepper to taste

Servings = 2

Mode of cooking: Grill

Procedure: Season the chicken breasts with salt and pepper. Grill the chicken breasts over medium heat for 6-7 minutes per side, or until cooked through.Allow the chicken to rest, then slice into strips.In a large bowl, toss the baby spinach and red onion with a drizzle of olive oil.Divide the dressed spinach onto two plates and top with the grilled chicken slices. Sprinkle with sliced almonds and serve.

Nutritional values: 410 calories | 46g protein | 24g fat | 5g carbohydrates

7.5 Fish and Seafood Medleys: From Sea to Plate

Recipe 1: Grilled Salmon with Lemon Butter

Preparation time = 15 minutes

Ingredients: 2 salmon filets | 2 tablespoons butter | 1 tablespoon lemon juice | Salt and pepper to taste

Servings = 2

Mode of cooking: Grill

Procedure: Preheat the grill to medium-high heat.Season the salmon filets with salt and pepper.Grill the salmon for 4-5 minutes on each side, or until flaky and cooked through.In a small saucepan, melt the butter and stir in the lemon juice.Pour the lemon butter over the grilled salmon filets before serving.

Nutritional values: 400 calories | 40g protein | 25g fat | 0g carbohydrates

Recipe 2: Shrimp Scampi

Preparation time = 20 minutes

Ingredients: 1 pound shrimp, peeled and deveined | 4 cloves garlic, minced | 1/4 cup butter | 1/4 cup white wine | Salt and pepper to taste

Servings = 2

Mode of cooking: Stovetop

Procedure: In a large skillet, melt the butter over medium heat.Add the minced garlic and cook for 1-2 minutes, until fragrant.Add the shrimp to the skillet and cook for 2-3 minutes per side, until pink and opaque.Pour in the white wine and allow it to simmer for another minute.Season with salt and pepper before serving.

Nutritional values: 320 calories | 38g protein | 18g fat | 3g carbohydrates

Recipe 3: Tuna Avocado Salad

Preparation time = 15 minutes

Ingredients: 2 cans of tuna, drained | 1 ripe avocado, diced | 2 tablespoons olive oil | 1 tablespoon lemon juice | Salt and pepper to taste

Servings = 2

Mode of cooking: No cooking required

Procedure: In a medium bowl, combine the drained tuna and diced avocado.Drizzle with olive oil and lemon juice, then season with salt and pepper. Gently toss to combine.

Nutritional values: 340 calories | 45g protein | 18g fat | 2g carbohydrates

Recipe 4: Grilled Swordfish Steak

Preparation time = 20 minutes

Ingredients: 2 swordfish steaks | 2 tablespoons olive oil | 1 teaspoon dried oregano | Salt and pepper to taste

Servings = 2

Mode of cooking: Grill

Procedure: Preheat the grill to medium-high heat.Rub the swordfish steaks with olive oil and season with oregano, salt, and pepper.Grill the swordfish for 5-6 minutes per side, or until it flakes easily with a fork.

Nutritional values: 380 calories | 42g protein | 22g fat | 0g carbohydrates

---

Recipe 5: Lemon Garlic Butter Scallops

Preparation time = 15 minutes

Ingredients: 1 pound sea scallops | 3 tablespoons butter | 2 cloves garlic, minced | 1 tablespoon lemon juice | Salt and pepper to taste

Servings = 2

Mode of cooking: Stovetop

Procedure: Pat the scallops dry and season with salt and pepper.In a large skillet, melt the butter over medium-high heat.Add the minced garlic and cook for 1 minute.Add the scallops to the skillet and cook for 2-3 minutes per side, until golden brown and opaque.Finish by squeezing lemon juice over the scallops before serving.

Nutritional values: 320 calories | 40g protein | 17g fat | 4g carbohydrate

---

Chapter 8: Dinner on the Wild Side: Carnivore Feasts

8.1 Steak Night Favorites: Grill Like a Pro

Recipe 1: Grilled Ribeye Steak with Garlic Butter

Preparation time = 15 minutes

Ingredients: 2 ribeye steaks | 2 tablespoons butter | 2 cloves garlic, minced | Salt and pepper to taste

Servings = 2

Mode of cooking: Grill

Procedure: Preheat the grill to high heat.Season the ribeye steaks with salt and pepper.Grill the steaks for 4-5 minutes on each side for medium-rare doneness.In a small saucepan, melt the butter and cook the minced garlic until fragrant.Pour the garlic butter over the grilled steaks before serving.

Nutritional values: 500 calories | 50g protein | 32g fat | 0g carbohydrates

Recipe 2: Pan-Seared Filet Mignon

Preparation time = 20 minutes

Ingredients: 2 filet mignon steaks | 2 tablespoons olive oil | Salt and pepper to taste

Servings = 2

Mode of cooking: Stovetop

Procedure: Heat the olive oil in a large skillet over high heat.Season the filet mignon steaks with salt and pepper.Sear the steaks for 3-4 minutes on each side for medium-rare doneness.

Nutritional values: 480 calories | 55g protein | 28g fat | 0g carbohydrates

Recipe 3: Garlic Herb Butter Striploin Steak

Preparation time = 15 minutes

Ingredients: 2 striploin steaks | 3 tablespoons butter | 2 cloves garlic, minced | 1 teaspoon chopped fresh herbs (such as rosemary or thyme) | Salt and pepper to taste

Servings = 2

Mode of cooking: Grill or stovetop

Procedure: Season the striploin steaks with salt and pepper.Grill or sear the steaks for 4-5 minutes on each side for medium-rare doneness.In a small saucepan, melt the butter and add the minced garlic and chopped herbs.Pour the garlic herb butter over the cooked steaks before serving.

Nutritional values: 520 calories | 45g protein | 38g fat | 0g carbohydrates

Recipe 4: T-Bone Steak with Chimichurri Sauce

Preparation time = 20 minutes

Ingredients: 2 T-bone steaks | 1/4 cup olive oil | 2 tablespoons red wine vinegar | 2 cloves garlic, minced | 2 tablespoons chopped fresh parsley | Salt and pepper to taste

Servings = 2

Mode of cooking: Grill

Procedure: In a small bowl, whisk together the olive oil, red wine vinegar, minced garlic, and chopped parsley to

make the chimichurri sauce.Season the T-bone steaks with salt and pepper.Grill the steaks for 5-6 minutes on each side for medium doneness.Serve the T-bone steaks with a generous drizzle of the chimichurri sauce on top.

Nutritional values: 540 calories | 55g protein | 34g fat | 1g carbohydrates

Recipe 5: Porterhouse Steak with Blue Cheese Butter

Preparation time = 20 minutes

Ingredients: 2 porterhouse steaks | 2 tablespoons butter | 2 tablespoons crumbled blue cheese | Salt and pepper to taste

Servings = 2

Mode of cooking: Grill or stovetop

Procedure: Season the porterhouse steaks with salt and pepper.Grill or sear the steaks for 5-6 minutes on each side for medium doneness.In a small bowl, mix together the butter and crumbled blue cheese to make the blue cheese butter.Place a dollop of the blue cheese butter on top of each cooked steak before serving.

Nutritional values: 580 calories | 60g protein | 40g fat | 0g carbohydrate

8.2 Slow-Cooked Meat Masterpieces: Set It and Forget It

Recipe 1: Slow-Cooked Beef Stew

Preparation time = 15 minutes

Ingredients : 2 lbs beef stew meat | 1 onion, diced | 2 cloves garlic, minced | 1 cup beef broth | salt | pepper

Servings = Serves 4

Mode of cooking: Slow cooker

Procedure: Place beef stew meat, diced onion, minced garlic, and beef broth in a slow cooker. Season with salt and pepper to taste. Cook on low heat for 8-10 hours. Serve hot.

Nutritional values: Approximately 300 calories | 40g protein | 15g fat | 0g carbohydrates

Recipe 2: Slow-Cooked Pork Shoulder

Preparation time = 10 minutes

Ingredients = 3 lbs pork shoulder | 2 tablespoons salt | 1 tablespoon black pepper | 1 tablespoon garlic powder

Servings = Serves 6

Mode of cooking: Slow cooker

Procedure: Season the pork shoulder with salt, black pepper, and garlic powder. Place it in a slow cooker on low heat for 8-10 hours. Shred the meat and serve.

Nutritional values: Approximately 400 calories | 30g protein | 25g fat | 0g carbohydrates

Recipe 3: Slow-Cooked Lamb Shanks

Preparation time = 20 minutes

Ingredients : 4 lamb shanks | rosemary | thyme | salt | pepper

Servings = Serves 4

Mode of cooking: Slow cooker

Procedure: Season the lamb shanks with rosemary, thyme, salt, and pepper. Place them in a slow cooker on low heat for 8-10 hours. Serve with the cooking liquid.

Nutritional values: Approximately 350 calories | 35g protein | 20g fat | 0g carbohydrates

Recipe 4: Slow-Cooked Chicken Drumsticks

Preparation time = 15 minutes

Ingredients = 8 chicken drumsticks | paprika | salt | pepper

Servings = Serves 4

Mode of cooking: Slow cooker

Procedure: Season the chicken drumsticks with paprika, salt, and pepper. Place them in a slow cooker on low heat for 4-6 hours. Serve hot.

Nutritional values: Approximately 250 calories | 30g protein | 15g fat | 0g carbohydrates

Recipe 5: Slow-Cooked Bison Roast

Preparation time = 20 minutes

Ingredients = 3 lbs bison roast | 1 onion, sliced | 2 cloves garlic, minced | 1 cup beef broth | salt | pepper

Servings = Serves 6

Mode of cooking: Slow cooker

Procedure: Place bison roast, sliced onion, minced garlic, and beef broth in a slow cooker. Season with salt and pepper to taste. Cook on low heat for 8-10 hours. Slice and serve.

Nutritional values: Approximately 300 calories | 40g protein | 10g fat | 0g carbohydrates.

8.3 Grilled and Smoked Delights: Summertime Sizzlers

Recipe 1: Smoked Beef Ribs

Preparation time = 30 minutes

Ingredients = 3 lbs beef ribs | smoked sea salt | black pepper

Servings = Serves 4

Mode of cooking: Smoker

Procedure: Season beef ribs with smoked sea salt and black pepper. Smoke at 225°F for 3-4 hours until tender.

Nutritional values: 400 calories | 35g protein | 30g fat | 0g carbohydrates

Recipe 2: Grilled Lamb Chops

Preparation time = 20 minutes

Ingredients = 8 lamb chops | garlic powder | rosemary | olive oil

Servings = Serves 4

Mode of cooking: Grill

Procedure: Season lamb chops with garlic powder, rosemary, and olive oil.

Grill over high heat for 4-5 minutes per side.

Nutritional values: 350 calories | 30g protein | 25g fat | 0g carbohydrates

Recipe 3: Smoked Pork Belly

Preparation time = 60 minutes

Ingredients : 2 lbs pork belly | cumin | paprika | salt

Servings = Serves 6

Mode of cooking: Smoker

Procedure: Rub pork belly with cumin, paprika, and salt. Smoke at 250°F for 2-3 hours until crispy.

Nutritional values: 450 calories | 20g protein | 40g fat | 0g carbohydrates

Recipe 4: Grilled Bison Steaks

Preparation time = 15 minutes

Ingredients :4 bison strip steaks | salt | black pepper

Servings = Serves 4

Mode of cooking: Grill

Procedure: Season bison steaks with salt and black pepper. Grill over medium-high heat for 3-4 minutes per side.

Nutritional values: 300 calories | 45g protein | 10g fat | 0g carbohydrates

---

Recipe 5: Smoked Chicken Thighs

Preparation time = 20 minutes

Ingredients : 8 chicken thighs | smoked paprika | garlic powder | olive oil

Servings = Serves 4

Mode of cooking: Smoker

Procedure: Season chicken thighs with smoked paprika, garlic powder, and olive oil. Smoke at 250°F for 1.5-2 hours until juicy.

Nutritional values: 250 calories | 30g protein | 15g fat | 0g carbohydrates

---

8.4 Organ Meat Specialties: Embracing Nose-to-Tail Eating

Recipe 1: Chicken Liver Pâté

Preparation time = 30 minutes

Ingredients : 1 lb chicken livers | 1/2 cup butter | 1 onion, chopped | 2 cloves garlic, minced

Servings = Serves 6

Mode of cooking: Stovetop

Procedure: Sauté chopped onions and minced garlic in butter until translucent. Add chicken livers and cook until fully cooked. Blend the mixture until smooth. Allow to cool, then refrigerate until set. Serve as a spread.

Nutritional values: 220 calories | 25g protein | 12g fat | 3g carbohydrates

Recipe 2: Grilled Beef Heart Skewers

Preparation time = 40 minutes

Ingredients : 2 lbs beef heart, cubed | 1/4 cup olive oil | 2 tablespoons balsamic vinegar | salt | pepper

Servings = Serves 4

Mode of cooking: Grill

Procedure: Marinate beef heart cubes in olive oil, balsamic vinegar, salt, and pepper for 30 minutes. Skewer the cubes and grill over medium-high heat for 4-5 minutes per side.

Nutritional values: 280 calories | 30g protein | 15g fat | 0g carbohydrates

Recipe 3: Pan-Seared Duck Hearts

Preparation time = 25 minutes

Ingredients: 1 lb duck hearts | 2 tablespoons ghee | fresh thyme | salt | black pepper

Servings = Serves 4

Mode of cooking: Stovetop

Procedure: Melt ghee in a skillet over medium-high heat. Season duck hearts with fresh thyme, salt, and pepper. Sear for 3-4 minutes per side until cooked to desired doneness.

Nutritional values: 240 calories | 28g protein | 14g fat | 0g carbohydrates

Recipe 4: Braised Lamb Tongue

Preparation time = 2 hours

Ingredients : 6 lamb tongues | 2 cups beef broth | 1 onion, sliced | 3 cloves garlic, crushed | bay leaf

Servings = Serves 4

Mode of cooking: Stovetop

Procedure: Place lamb tongues, sliced onion, crushed garlic, and bay leaf in a pot. Add beef broth. Bring to a boil, then reduce heat and simmer for 1.5-2 hours until tender. Serve sliced with cooking liquid.

Nutritional values: 320 calories | 25g protein | 22g fat | 0g carbohydrates

Recipe 5: Beef Kidney Stir-Fry

Preparation time = 30 minutes

Ingredients : 2 beef kidneys, sliced | 1 bell pepper, sliced | 1 onion, sliced | 2 tablespoons coconut aminos

Servings = Serves 4

Mode of cooking: Stovetop

Procedure: In a skillet, sauté beef kidneys, bell pepper, and onion over medium heat. Add coconut aminos and cook for 10-15 minutes until the kidneys are tender. Serve hot.

Nutritional values: 250 calories | 20g protein | 15g fat | 5g carbohydrates

---

8.5 Surf and Turf Combos: The Best of Both Worlds

Recipe 1: Grilled Ribeye Steak with Garlic Shrimp

Preparation time = 30 minutes

Ingredients : 2 ribeye steaks (1 inch thick) | 1 lb shrimp, peeled and deveined | 3 cloves garlic, minced | 2 tablespoons olive oil

Servings = Serves 2

Mode of cooking: Grill

Procedure: Season ribeye steaks with salt and pepper. Grill over high heat for 4-5 minutes per side for medium-rare. In a separate pan, heat olive oil and sauté minced garlic for 1 minute. Add shrimp and cook for 2-3 minutes until pink and cooked through. Serve the grilled steak with garlic shrimp on the side.

Nutritional values: 700 calories | 60g protein | 45g fat | 2g carbohydrates

---

Recipe 2: Pan-Seared Filet Mignon and Lobster Tail

Preparation time = 35 minutes

Ingredients :2 filet mignon steaks (6 oz each) | 2 lobster tails | 2 tablespoons butter | salt | pepper

Servings = Serves 2

Mode of cooking: Stovetop/Oven

Procedure: Preheat the oven to 400°F. Season filet mignon steaks with salt and pepper. In a skillet, heat butter over medium-high heat and sear the steaks for 2-3 minutes on each side. Transfer the steaks to a baking sheet and cook in the preheated oven for 8-10 minutes for medium-rare.Meanwhile, split the lobster tails lengthwise and season with salt and pepper. Grill or broil the lobster tails for 6-8 minutes until the meat is opaque. Serve the filet mignon with a lobster tail on top.

Nutritional values: 650 calories | 55g protein | 40g fat | 0g carbohydrates

Recipe 3:Grilled T-Bone Steak and Scallops

Preparation time = 40 minutes

Ingredients :2 T-bone steaks (1 inch thick) | 1 lb scallops | 2 tablespoons olive oil | salt | pepper

Servings = Serves 2

Mode of cooking: Grill

Procedure: Season T-bone steaks with salt and pepper. Grill over high heat for 5-6 minutes per side for medium doneness. In a separate pan, heat olive oil over medium-high heat. Season scallops with salt and pepper, then sear them for 2-3 minutes on each side until golden brown. Serve the grilled T-bone steak with seared scallops on the side.

Nutritional values: 600 calories | 60g protein | 35g fat | 0g carbohydrates

Recipe 4: Bacon-Wrapped Filet Mignon and Grilled Shrimp Skewers

Preparation time = 45 minutes

Ingredients : 2 filet mignon steaks (6 oz each) | 1 lb large shrimp, peeled and deveined | 4 slices bacon | salt | pepper

Servings = Serves 2

Mode of cooking: Grill

Procedure: Wrap each filet mignon steak with 2 slices of bacon and secure with toothpicks. Season with salt and pepper. Grill over medium-high heat for 5-6 minutes per side for medium-rare. Thread the peeled shrimp on skewers and grill for 3-4 minutes per side until pink and cooked through. Serve the bacon-wrapped filet mignon with grilled shrimp skewers on the side.

Nutritional values: 700 calories | 55g protein | 45g fat | 0g carbohydrates

Recipe 5: Grilled Porterhouse Steak and Garlic Butter Lobster

Preparation time = 40 minutes

Ingredients : 1 Porterhouse steak (1.5 lb) | 2 lobster tails | 4 tablespoons butter | 4 cloves garlic, minced | salt | pepper

Servings = Serves 2

Mode of cooking: Grill/Oven/Stovetop

Procedure: Preheat the grill to high heat. Season the Porterhouse steak with salt and pepper. Grill for 5-6 minutes per side for medium-rare. Meanwhile, split the lobster tails lengthwise and season with salt and pepper. Melt butter in a skillet over medium heat, then add minced garlic and sauté for 1 minute. Add the lobster tails, flesh side down, and cook for 3-4 minutes until the meat is opaque and cooked through. Serve the grilled Porterhouse steak with garlic butter lobster on the side.

Nutritional values: 850 calories | 75g protein | 55g fat | 0g carbohydrates

Chapter 9: Snack Attack: Carnivore-Friendly Munchies

9.1 Beef Jerky and Biltong: Portable Protein Powerhouses

Recipe 1: Classic Beef Jerky

Preparation time= 15 minutes

Ingredients: 1 pound beef top round, thinly sliced | ¼ cup coconut aminos | 1 teaspoon onion powder | 1 teaspoon garlic powder

Servings= Serves 4

Mode of cooking: Dehydrator

Procedure: Marinate beef slices in a mixture of coconut aminos, onion powder, and garlic powder. Dehydrate at 160°F for 4-6 hours.

Nutritional values: approximately 160 calories | 22g protein | 7g fat | 1g carb

Recipe 2: Spicy Biltong Sticks

Preparation time= 20 minutes

Ingredients: 1 pound beef silverside or eye of round, thinly sliced | 2 tablespoons apple cider vinegar | 1 tablespoon paprika | 1 teaspoon cayenne pepper

Servings= Serves 6

Mode of cooking: Air-dried

Procedure: Coat beef slices in a spice mix of apple cider vinegar, paprika, and cayenne pepper. Air-dry in a cool, dry place for 3-5 days.

Nutritional values: approximately 140 calories | 18g protein | 6g fat | 1g carb

Recipe 3: Garlic Pepper Beef Jerky

Preparation time=15 minutes

Ingredients: 1 pound beef sirloin, thinly sliced | ¼ cup coconut aminos | 2 cloves garlic, minced | 1 teaspoon black pepper

Servings= Serves 4

Mode of cooking: Dehydrator

Procedure: Marinate beef slices in a mixture of coconut aminos, minced garlic, and black pepper. Dehydrate at 160°F for 5-7 hours.

Nutritional values: approximately 170 calories | 23g protein | 6g fat | 2g carb

---

Recipe 4: Herb-Infused Biltong Strips

Preparation time= 20 minutes

Ingredients: 1 pound beef topside, thinly sliced | 2 tablespoons apple cider vinegar | 1 tablespoon dried mixed herbs | Salt to taste

Servings= Serves 6

Mode of cooking: Air-dried

Procedure: Combine beef strips with apple cider vinegar, mixed herbs, and salt. Hang in a well-ventilated area to air-dry for 3-4 days.

Nutritional values: approximately 150 calories | 20g protein | 5g fat | 1g carb

---

Recipe 5: Teriyaki Beef Jerky

Preparation time=15 minutes

Ingredients: 1 pound beef flank steak, thinly sliced | ¼ cup coconut aminos | 1 tablespoon grated ginger | 1 tablespoon sesame seeds

Servings= Serves 4

Mode of cooking: Dehydrator

Procedure: Marinate beef slices in coconut aminos, grated ginger, and sesame seeds. Dehydrate at 160°F for 4-6 hours.

Nutritional values: approximately 180 calories | 24g protein | 7g fat | 2g carb

---

9.2 Pork Rinds and Cracklings: Crispy, Crunchy, and Addictive

Recipe 1: Classic Pork Rinds

Preparation time= 10 minutes

Ingredients: 1 pound pork skin | Salt to taste

Servings= Serves 8

Mode of cooking: Oven-baked

Procedure: Cut pork skin into bite-sized pieces. Season with salt. Bake in a preheated 400°F oven for 15-20 minutes until crispy.

Nutritional values: approximately 90 calories | 9g protein | 6g fat | 0g carb

Recipe 2: Spicy Pork Cracklings

Preparation time= 15 minutes

Ingredients: **1** pound pork belly, skin-on | 1 tablespoon chili powder | 1 teaspoon paprika | Salt to taste

Servings= Serves 6

Mode of cooking: Stovetop

Procedure: Cut pork belly into small pieces. Place in a skillet and cook over medium heat until the fat is rendered and the skin becomes crispy. Season with chili powder, paprika, and salt.

Nutritional values: approximately 120 calories | 8g protein | 9g fat | 0g carb

Recipe 3: Garlic Parmesan Pork Rinds

Preparation time= 15 minutes

Ingredients: 1 pound pork skin | 2 tablespoons grated parmesan cheese | 1 teaspoon garlic powder

Servings= Serves 8

Mode of cooking: Air-fried

Procedure: Cut pork skin into strips. Toss with grated parmesan cheese and garlic powder. Air-fry at 400°F for 10-12 minutes until golden and crispy.

Nutritional values: approximately 100 calories | 10g protein | 7g fat | 0g carb

Recipe 4: Rosemary Salted Pork Cracklings

Preparation time= 20 minutes

Ingredients: 1 pound pork belly, skin-on | 2 tablespoons chopped fresh rosemary | Salt to taste

Servings= Serves 6

Mode of cooking: Oven-baked

Procedure: Cut pork belly into small pieces. Season with chopped fresh rosemary and salt. Roast in a preheated 375°F oven for 25-30 minutes until crunchy.

Nutritional values: approximately 110 calories | 7g protein | 8g fat | 0g carb

Recipe 5: BBQ Seasoned Pork Rinds

Preparation time= 15 minutes

Ingredients: 1 pound pork skin | 2 tablespoons BBQ seasoning

Servings= Serves 8

Mode of cooking: Dehydrator

Procedure: Cut pork skin into squares. Toss with BBQ seasoning. Dehydrate at 160°F for 4-6 hours until crispy.

Nutritional values: approximately 95 calories | 9g protein | 6g fat | 0g carb

9.3 Hard-Boiled Egg Variations: Nature's Perfect Snack

Recipe 1: Classic Hard-Boiled Eggs

Preparation time= 15 minutes

Ingredients: 6 large eggs

Servings= Serves 3

Mode of cooking: Stovetop

Procedure: Place eggs in a saucepan and cover with water. Bring to a boil, then cover and remove from heat. Let stand for 10-12 minutes. Plunge into cold water and peel.

Nutritional values: approximately 70 calories | 6g protein | 5g fat | 0.5g carb

Recipe 2: Herb-Crusted Hard-Boiled Eggs

Preparation time= 20 minutes

Ingredients: 6 large eggs | 2 tablespoons chopped fresh herbs (parsley, dill, chives) | Salt and pepper to taste

Servings= Serves 3

Mode of cooking: Stovetop

Procedure: Boil the eggs, then roll them in the chopped herbs, salt, and pepper for a flavorful twist on a classic snack.

Nutritional values: approximately 75 calories | 6g protein | 6g fat | 0.5g carb

Recipe 3: Bacon-Wrapped Hard-Boiled Eggs

Preparation time= 25 minutes

Ingredients: 6 large eggs | 6 slices of bacon

Servings: Serves 3

Mode of cooking: Oven-baked

Procedure: Wrap hard-boiled eggs with bacon and bake at 400°F for 15-20 minutes until the bacon is crispy.

Nutritional values: approximately 120 calories | 9g protein | 9g fat | 0.5g carb

Recipe 4: Curry-Spiced Hard-Boiled Eggs

Preparation time= 20 minutes

Ingredients: 6 large eggs | 1 tablespoon curry powder | Salt to taste

Servings: Serves 3

Mode of cooking: Stovetop

Procedure: Peel the hard-boiled eggs and slice them in half. Sprinkle it with curry powder and salt for an exotic flavor.

Nutritional values: approximately 80 calories | 6g protein | 6g fat | 0.5g carb

Ingredients: 6 large eggs | 2 teaspoons smoked paprika | Salt to taste

Servings= Serves 3

Mode of cooking: Stovetop

Procedure: Peel the hard-boiled eggs and sprinkle with smoked paprika and salt for a smoky, savory snack.

Nutritional values: approximately 75 calories | 6g protein | 6g fat | 0.5g carb

Recipe 5: Smoked Paprika Hard-Boiled Eggs

Preparation time= 15 minutes

9.4 Canned Fish Snacks: Convenient and Nutritious

Recipe 1: Tuna Stuffed Avocado

Preparation time= 10 minutes

Ingredients: 1 can of tuna, drained | 2 ripe avocados | Salt and pepper to taste

Servings= Serves 2

Mode of preparation: No cooking required

Procedure: Cut the avocados in half and remove the pit. Fill the hollow of each avocado half with canned tuna. Season with salt and pepper.

Nutritional values: approximately 250 calories | 25g protein | 15g fat | 7g carb

Recipe 2: Sardine Lettuce Wraps

Preparation time: 10 minutes

Ingredients: 1 can of sardines in olive oil | 6 large lettuce leaves | Mustard or hot sauce (optional)

Servings=Serves 2

Mode of preparation: No cooking required

Procedure: Lay out the lettuce leaves and place sardines in each leaf. Add mustard or hot sauce for extra flavor, if desired. Roll up and enjoy.

Nutritional values: approximately 200 calories | 20g protein | 10g fat | 2g carb

Recipe 3: Salmon Cucumber Bites

Preparation time: 15 minutes

Ingredients: 1 can of wild-caught salmon, drained | 1 large cucumber, sliced | Dill for garnish

Servings= Serves 4

Mode of preparation: No cooking required

Procedure: Top cucumber slices with canned salmon and garnish with dill for a refreshing and protein-packed snack.

Nutritional values: approximately 180 calories | 20g protein | 9g fat | 5g carb

Recipe 4: Anchovy Stuffed Eggs

Preparation time=20 minutes

Ingredients: 1 can of anchovy fillets | 6 hard-boiled eggs | Chives for garnish

Servings= Serves 3

Mode of preparation: No cooking required

Procedure: Cut the hard-boiled eggs in half and remove the yolks. Fill the hollow of each egg half with an anchovy filet. Garnish with chives.

Nutritional values: approximately 160 calories | 12g protein | 10g fat | 3g carb

Ingredients: 1 can of mackerel, drained | 8 large cabbage leaves | Lemon wedges for serving

Servings= Serves 4

Mode of preparation: No cooking required

Procedure: Place mackerel on cabbage leaves and serve with lemon wedges for a simple and nutritious snack.

Nutritional values: approximately 220 calories | 25g protein | 12g fat | 6g carb

Recipe 5: Mackerel Cabbage Cups

Preparation time=15 minutes

9.5 Bone Broth Sippers: Nourishing Elixirs for Any Time of Day

Recipe 1: Classic Beef Bone Broth

Preparation time= 12 hours

Ingredients: 2 lbs beef marrow bones | Water | Salt to taste

Servings= Makes 8 cups

Mode of cooking: Slow cooker or stovetop

Procedure: Place bones in a pot, cover with water, and simmer on low heat for 12 hours. Add salt to taste and strain before serving.

Nutritional values: approximately 50 calories | 8g protein | 2g fat | 0g carb

Recipe 2: Turkey Bone Broth with Herbs

Preparation time= 10 hours

Ingredients: 2 lbs turkey bones | 1 onion, chopped | Fresh herbs (rosemary, thyme) | Water

Servings= Makes 6 cups

Mode of cooking: Slow cooker or stovetop

Procedure: Combine all ingredients in a slow cooker. Cook on low for 10 hours. Strain and serve.

Nutritional values: approximately 40 calories | 7g protein | 1g fat | 0g carb

Recipe 3: Lamb Bone Broth with Garlic

Preparation time= 15 hours

Ingredients: 2 lbs lamb bones | 3 cloves garlic, crushed | Water | Salt to taste

Servings= Makes 10 cups

Mode of cooking: Slow cooker or stovetop

Procedure: Place lamb bones and garlic in a pot, cover with water, and cook on low heat for 15 hours.

Nutritional values: approximately 60 calories | 9g protein | 3g fat | 0g carb

Recipe 4: Chicken Bone Broth with Turmeric

Preparation time=8 hours

Ingredients: 2 lbs chicken bones | 1 tablespoon turmeric powder | Water

Servings= Makes 8 cups

Mode of cooking: Slow cooker or stovetop

Procedure: Combine all ingredients in a pot or slow cooker. Cook on low for 8 hours. Strain and enjoy the nourishing elixir.

Nutritional values: approximately 35 calories | 6g protein | 1g fat | 0g carb

Recipe 5: Pork Bone Broth with Apple Cider Vinegar

Preparation time=14 hours

Ingredients: 2 lbs pork bones | 2 tablespoons apple cider vinegar | Water

Servings= Makes 9 cups

Mode of cooking: Slow cooker or stovetop

Procedure: Place pork bones in a pot, add apple cider vinegar, cover with water, and simmer on low heat for 14 hours. Strain and sip on this nourishing broth.

Nutritional values: approximately 55 calories | 8g protein | 2.5g fat | 0g carb

Chapter 10: Troubleshooting and FAQs

10.1 Overcoming Plateaus and Stalls

When embarking on a new dietary journey, it's common to experience plateaus and stalls, where your progress seems to slow down or come to a halt. It's important to understand that this is a normal part of the process as your body adjusts to the new way of eating. Here are some strategies to overcome plateaus and stalls on the carnivore diet.

Understanding Your Body's Adaptation

First and foremost, it's crucial to understand that your body is undergoing a significant adaptation process as you transition to the carnivore diet. Your metabolism, hormone levels, and gut microbiome are all adjusting to the new way of eating. This adaptation period can lead to fluctuations in weight loss and energy levels, which may manifest as plateaus or stalls.

Stay Consistent and Patient

Consistency is key when it comes to overcoming plateaus and stalls. Stick to the carnivore diet and give your body the time it needs to adapt. Remember that every individual's journey is unique, and progress may not always follow a linear trajectory. Be patient and trust the process.

Reassess Your Macros

If you've hit a plateau or stall, it may be worth reassessing your macronutrient intake. Ensure that you're consuming adequate protein to support muscle maintenance and overall metabolic function. Adjust your fat intake based on your energy levels and satiety. Experiment with varying your fat-to-protein ratio to see how your body responds.

Incorporate Intermittent Fasting

Intermittent fasting can be a valuable tool for breaking through plateaus and stalls. By extending the fasting window between meals, you give your body the opportunity to tap into stored fat for energy. This approach can revitalize your metabolism and kick start fat loss.

Explore Exercise and Movement

Physical activity can provide the necessary stimulus to overcome plateaus and stalls. Incorporate strength training or high-intensity interval exercises to build lean muscle mass and boost your metabolism. Additionally, regular movement throughout the day, such as walking or light physical activities, can contribute to overall energy expenditure.

Consider Stress and Sleep

Stress management and quality sleep are often overlooked factors in overcoming plateaus and stalls. Chronic stress can lead to hormonal imbalances that impact weight loss and overall well-being. Prioritize relaxation techniques, such as meditation or deep breathing exercises, to mitigate stress. Aim for sufficient, restorative sleep to support your body's adaptive processes.

Seek Professional Guidance

If you've diligently implemented these strategies and still find yourself struggling with plateaus and stalls, consider consulting a healthcare professional or a registered dietitian with experience in the carnivore diet. They can offer personalized guidance and support to help you navigate through challenging phases and optimize your dietary approach.

Ultimately, overcoming plateaus and stalls on the carnivore diet requires a combination of patience, consistency, and an understanding of your body's unique adaptation process.

10.2 Dealing with Cravings

Cravings can be a significant challenge when adopting a new diet, especially one as unique as the carnivore diet. The transition from a diet rich in carbohydrates and sugars to one focused solely on animal-based foods may lead to cravings for familiar and comforting foods. However, understanding the root causes of these cravings and implementing effective strategies can help you overcome them and stay on track with your carnivore lifestyle.

Understanding the Nature of Cravings

Cravings often arise from a combination of physical and psychological factors. Physiologically, cravings can be attributed to fluctuations in blood sugar levels, imbalances in hormonal signaling, or even nutrient deficiencies. On the psychological front, cravings can stem from emotional triggers, such as stress, boredom, or habit. Recognizing the underlying triggers can help you address cravings more effectively.

Balancing Blood Sugar Levels

One of the main culprits behind cravings is unstable blood sugar levels. When you consume carbohydrates, your body breaks them down into glucose, causing a spike in blood sugar. This surge is followed by a rapid drop in blood sugar, triggering cravings as your body seeks quick sources of energy. By eliminating carbohydrates from your diet, the carnivore diet helps stabilize blood sugar levels, reducing the intensity and frequency of cravings.

Optimizing Nutrient Intake

In some cases, cravings can be a sign of nutritional deficiencies. As you transition to the carnivore diet, it's essential to ensure you're consuming a variety of animal-based foods to meet your body's nutritional needs. Different animal products offer unique profiles of vitamins, minerals, and other essential nutrients. Incorporating a range of meats, fish, organs, and eggs can help minimize cravings driven by nutrient imbalances.

Managing Psychological Triggers

While the carnivore diet addresses many physiological aspects of cravings, it's important to address the psychological triggers as well. Find alternative ways to cope with stress or boredom to minimize the likelihood of turning to food for comfort. Engaging in activities you enjoy, practicing mindfulness or meditation, or seeking emotional support can provide healthier paths to address emotional triggers without relying on food.

Experimenting with Food Varieties and Cooking Techniques

To make the carnivore diet more enjoyable and satisfy cravings, it's crucial to explore different types of animal-based foods and experiment with cooking techniques. The world of meats, fish, and poultry is vast and diverse, offering a multitude of flavors and textures. By broadening your culinary horizons, you can find new favorites and creative ways to prepare meals that satisfy cravings while adhering to the principles of the carnivore diet.

Finding Carnivore-Friendly Alternatives

Cravings for familiar non-carnivorous foods may still arise occasionally. In such instances, seeking carnivore-friendly alternatives can help alleviate cravings while maintaining the integrity of your dietary choices. For example, finding a tasty homemade jerky or biltong recipe can satisfy a craving for a snack while adhering to the principles of the carnivore diet. The focus should be on finding options that align with the core principles of your carnivorous approach.

Developing Mental Resilience

Dealing with cravings requires mental resilience and a long-term perspective. Remind yourself of the reasons you embarked on the carnivore diet journey and the goals you aspire to achieve. Embrace the benefits you have experienced so far and appreciate the positive changes taking place in your body. Developing a strong mindset will empower you to overcome cravings and stay committed to your carnivore lifestyle.

By understanding the nature of cravings, optimizing your nutrient intake, managing psychological triggers, experimenting with different foods, and developing mental resilience, you can effectively navigate cravings while following the carnivore diet.

10.3 Managing Constipation

Constipation is a common concern when transitioning to the carnivore diet. This issue arises due to the significant reduction in fiber intake, which can slow down digestion and bowel movements. To effectively manage constipation and ensure a smooth transition to the carnivore lifestyle, consider the following strategies:

Hydration Is Key

Hydration: Adequate water intake is crucial for maintaining healthy digestion. Make sure to drink plenty of water throughout the day to keep your digestive system running smoothly. Water helps soften the stool, making it easier to pass.

Focus on Electrolytes

Electrolytes: When increasing your meat consumption, it's essential to pay attention to your electrolyte balance. Electrolytes, such as sodium, potassium, and magnesium, play a vital role in maintaining proper muscle function, including the muscles of the digestive tract. Incorporate electrolyte-rich foods like bone broth and salted meats to support bowel function.

Include Organ Meats

Organ Meats: Organ meats, such as liver and kidney, are nutrient powerhouses that can aid in digestion. These meats are rich in vitamins and minerals, including vitamin B12 and iron, which support overall gut health and function. Incorporating organ meats into your carnivore meals can help alleviate constipation.

Try Natural Remedies

Natural Remedies: Certain natural remedies can help relieve constipation. For example, consuming magnesium-rich foods like spinach or taking a magnesium supplement can promote bowel regularity. Additionally, herbal teas such as peppermint or ginger tea can have a soothing effect on the digestive system.

Monitor Your Fat Intake

Fat Intake: While fats are a significant component of the carnivore diet, excessive fat consumption can sometimes lead to digestive issues, including constipation. Be mindful of your fat intake and consider adjusting the ratio of fat to protein in your meals if constipation persists.

Exercise Regularly

Regular Exercise: Physical activity is essential for promoting healthy digestion. Regular exercise helps stimulate bowel movements and can alleviate constipation. Incorporate activities like walking, yoga, or strength training into your daily routine to support overall gut health.

Consult a Healthcare Provider

If constipation persists despite implementing these strategies, it may be beneficial to consult with a healthcare provider or a qualified nutritionist. They can offer personalized guidance and recommendations to address your specific concerns and optimize your carnivore diet experience.

By implementing these practical tips and strategies, you can effectively manage constipation while enjoying the numerous health benefits of the carnivore diet.

10.4 Optimizing Sleep

Getting enough good-quality sleep is essential to our overall health and well-being. In our busy lives, it can be easy to sacrifice sleep in favor of getting more work done or having more leisure time. However, neglecting sleep can have serious consequences for our physical and mental health, as well as our ability to maintain a healthy weight and perform daily tasks.

The carnivore diet can actually improve sleep quality due to its ability to regulate blood sugar and hormonal levels. When we eat a diet high in processed carbohydrates and sugar, we experience fluctuations in blood sugar levels, which can disrupt our sleep and lead to waking up feeling groggy and tired.

In addition, the high levels of protein and healthy fats in the carnivore diet can promote the production of serotonin, a neurotransmitter that helps regulate mood and sleep. A diet lacking in protein can lead to low levels of serotonin and difficulty falling or staying asleep.

It is important to establish a regular sleep routine and stick to it, even on the weekends. Our bodies thrive on routine and consistency, and by going to bed and waking up at the same time every day, we can establish healthy sleeping habits.

Creating a relaxing sleep environment can also improve sleep quality. Ensure that your bedroom is dark, quiet, and cool, and avoid using electronic devices before bedtime. The blue light emitted by electronic devices can suppress the production of melatonin, a hormone that regulates sleep and wake cycles.

If you continue to struggle with getting enough sleep, there are several other strategies that you can try. These include taking a warm bath or shower before bed, listening to calming music or white noise, practicing relaxation techniques such as deep breathing or yoga, and avoiding caffeine or alcohol in the evening.

If you experience persistent sleep problems, it is important to speak with your healthcare provider, as these issues could be related to an underlying medical condition.

10.5 Answers to Frequently Asked Questions

In this section, we will address some commonly asked questions about the Carnivore Diet to provide a comprehensive understanding of the principles and practical aspects of this dietary approach. We will dispel myths, provide reassuring answers, and offer guidance to those who are considering or following the Carnivore Diet.

Q: Is the Carnivore Diet safe?

A: The Carnivore Diet is considered safe for the majority of individuals. It is important to note that as with any dietary change, consulting with a healthcare professional is advisable, particularly for those with pre-existing health conditions. While the emphasis on animal-based foods may raise concerns about nutrient deficiencies, the diet is designed to provide adequate nutrition. By choosing a variety of meats, organ meats, and seafood, along with the inclusion of eggs and some dairy products, you can meet your body's nutritional needs.

Q: Can the absence of plant foods lead to nutrient deficiencies?

A: While plant foods are often promoted as essential sources of vitamins, minerals, and fiber, the Carnivore Diet challenges this belief. Animal-based foods provide highly bioavailable nutrients that are easily absorbed by our bodies. Additionally, organ meats, such as liver and kidney, are rich in essential vitamins and minerals. By strategically selecting a diverse range of animal products, you can ensure nutrient adequacy and reduce the risk of deficiencies.

Q: Won't a high intake of saturated fats from animal foods increase the risk of heart disease?

A: The relationship between saturated fats and heart disease has been questioned in recent years. Contrary to previous beliefs, recent research suggests that saturated fats may not be as harmful as once thought. The Carnivore Diet prioritizes natural, unprocessed animal fats, which contain a balanced ratio of saturated, monounsaturated, and polyunsaturated fats. It is worth noting that this diet encourages the elimination of processed foods and refined vegetable oils – the true culprits behind heart disease.

Q: What about fiber? Won't the absence of plant foods lead to digestive issues?

A: Fiber has long been associated with digestive health, but it may not be as essential as commonly believed. Our bodies are well-equipped to digest and absorb animal-based foods efficiently. In fact, the absence of fiber can bring relief to individuals who experience gastrointestinal discomfort. As long as you are consuming an appropriate amount of water, the Carnivore Diet can promote healthy digestion and alleviate issues such as bloating and constipation.

Q: How can I maintain my energy levels without consuming carbohydrates?

A: The body has the remarkable ability to adapt and utilize alternative fuel sources. On the Carnivore Diet, your body undergoes a metabolic shift known as ketosis – a state where fats, including body fat, are efficiently burned for energy. As your body becomes accustomed to this metabolic state, you will likely experience increased energy levels and improved mental clarity. Many people find that they no longer experience the energy crashes associated with carbohydrate-dependent diets.

Q: Can the Carnivore Diet help with weight loss?

A: Yes, the Carnivore Diet can be an effective tool for weight loss. By eliminating processed carbohydrates and sugars, you reduce insulin spikes that trigger fat storage. The increased protein and fat intake on the Carnivore Diet helps you feel satiated and can naturally reduce calorie consumption. Additionally, the diet promotes the utilization of stored body fat for energy, leading to sustainable weight loss.

Q: How do I handle social situations and explain my diet to others?

A: Social pressures can be a common challenge when following a unique dietary approach. It's important to remember that your health and well-being are your top priorities. When faced with questions or criticism, kindly explain your reasons for choosing the Carnivore Diet and how it has positively impacted your life. If attending a social gathering, you can eat beforehand or bring a meat-based dish to share, ensuring that you have options aligned with your dietary choices.

Q: Are there any potential side effects or challenges when starting the Carnivore Diet?

A: While some individuals transition smoothly to the Carnivore Diet, others may experience a period of adaptation. Potential side effects during this phase include fatigue, headache, and digestive changes. These symptoms are often temporary and known as the "keto flu." To alleviate discomfort, staying hydrated, consuming adequate electrolytes, and gradually reducing carbohydrate intake can be helpful. Patience and perseverance are key during this adjustment period.

The Carnivore Diet offers a unique approach to resolving health concerns and achieving weight loss goals. By focusing on animal-based foods and eliminating carbohydrates and plant foods, individuals may experience improved energy levels, weight loss, and relief from various health issues.

Chapter 11: Carnivore Diet Success Stories

11.1 John's 100-Pound Weight Loss Triumph

In this chapter, we dive into the inspiring success stories of individuals who have experienced significant transformations through the carnivore diet. These stories serve as powerful examples of how embracing the carnivore lifestyle can lead to remarkable health improvements and weight loss. One such success story is that of John, who achieved a remarkable 100-pound weight loss on the carnivore diet.

John's journey began like many others, with frustration and dissatisfaction with traditional diets that left him feeling exhausted and overweight despite his attempts to eat healthily and exercise. After hearing about the carnivore diet and its potential to improve his health, John decided to give it a try. Little did he know that this decision would change his life forever.

Embarking on the carnivore diet, John experienced a profound shift in his understanding of nutrition and the role it plays in his overall well-being. No longer limited by restrictive calorie counting or the constant worry of food choices, he found a new freedom in embracing the simplicity of the carnivore diet. For John, this meant a focus on meat, fish, and eggs while eliminating sugars, grains, and even fruit and vegetables.

As John committed to following the carnivore diet, he began to witness incredible changes in his body and overall health. The first notable transformation was his weight loss. By adhering to the carnivore lifestyle and adopting healthy eating habits, John was able to shed an impressive 100 pounds. This drastic change not only improved his physical appearance but also had a profound impact on his self-confidence and overall sense of well-being.

Beyond weight loss, John also experienced numerous other health benefits. His energy levels soared, and he found himself feeling more vibrant and alive than ever before. Mental clarity became the norm, paving the way for increased focus and productivity in all aspects of his life. John also noticed a reduction in inflammation and pain, allowing him to move more freely and engage in physical activities that were previously challenging.

The carnivore diet brought about improvements in John's digestion and gut health as well. He no longer experienced the discomfort and bloating that had plagued him in the past. This newfound improvement in his digestion further fueled his commitment to the carnivore lifestyle.

John's success with the carnivore diet goes beyond physical transformations. It also brought about a profound shift in his mindset and overall outlook on life. Through reconnecting with a more primitive and authentic way of eating, John felt a sense of vitality and authenticity that he had been missing. The carnivore diet allowed him to break free from the complications and pressures of modern society's dietary norms and embrace a more natural approach to nourishment.

John's success story serves as a beacon of hope for anyone looking to improve their health, lose weight, and increase energy levels. It highlights the incredible possibilities that lie within the carnivore diet when paired with dedication, commitment, and a desire for change.

11.2 How Sarah Reversed Her Autoimmune Disease

Sarah was a 38-year-old woman who had suffered from autoimmune disease for more than a decade. She had tried many different diets and treatments, but none had provided lasting relief from her symptoms. Her autoimmune disease had left her feeling fatigued, irritable, and in constant pain. After hearing about the carnivore diet, she decided to give it a try.

At first, Sarah was skeptical. How could a diet consisting of only meat, fish, and eggs help with her autoimmune disease? But as she began to research the science behind the diet, she realized that it was a promising approach. The carnivore diet emphasizes the elimination of plant foods that can potentially trigger autoimmune reactions in some people. Instead, the diet focuses on nutrient-dense animal foods that can support the body's natural healing processes.

After just a few weeks on the carnivore diet, Sarah began to notice a difference. Her joint pain and inflammation subsided, and she had more energy than she had in years. She continued with the diet for several months, gradually reintroducing some plant foods to her diet while still maintaining a focus on animal foods.

Over time, Sarah's autoimmune disease went into remission, and she was able to live a life free from the constant pain and fatigue that had plagued her for so long. She continued to follow the principles of the carnivore diet and eventually became an advocate for the diet and its potential benefits.

Sarah's success story highlights the potential benefits of the carnivore diet for people with autoimmune disease. While individual results may vary, many people have reported significant improvement in their symptoms after adopting a meat-based approach to eating. The key to success is to focus on nutrient-dense animal foods and to eliminate or severely restrict potentially triggering plant foods.

The carnivore diet may also be helpful for people with other chronic health conditions, such as type 2 diabetes, obesity, and gastrointestinal disorders. By eliminating processed foods, sugars, and refined carbohydrates, the diet can help improve insulin sensitivity, promote weight loss, and reduce inflammation.

However, it is important to note that the carnivore diet is not a one-size-fits-all solution. It may not be appropriate for certain populations, such as pregnant or breastfeeding women, people with kidney disease, or those with a history of eating disorders. It is also important to work with a healthcare practitioner to ensure that nutrient needs are being met and to monitor for potential side effects.

Sarah's success story demonstrates the potential benefits of the carnivore diet for people with autoimmune disease. The diet's emphasis on nutrient-dense animal foods and elimination of potentially triggering plant foods may promote healing and reduce inflammation.

11.3 Michael's Journey from Couch Potato to Athlete

Michael's story is a powerful testament to the transformative impact of the carnivore diet on one's physical health and overall well-being. As a 42-year-old man residing in a suburban neighborhood, Michael was no stranger to the frustrations and disappointments of traditional diets. Battling with excess weight, lack of energy, and a sedentary lifestyle, he felt trapped in a cycle of failed attempts to attain optimal health. However, everything changed when he embraced the carnivore diet, marking a remarkable and inspiring journey from couch potato to athlete.

At age 35, Michael's health was on a downward trajectory. With a demanding job and a sedentary lifestyle, he struggled with excess weight and a constant feeling of fatigue. Traditional diets seemed to offer only temporary relief, leaving him disheartened and skeptical about the possibility of achieving lasting transformation. However, his introduction to the carnivore diet sparked a drastic shift in his perspective.

Driven by a yearning for a radical and effective solution, Michael decided to embark on the carnivore diet journey. His primary aim was to shed excess weight and regain the vitality he felt was slipping away. Michael's journey began with a meticulous focus on sourcing quality animal products and eliminating all plant-based foods from his diet. The initial phase posed challenges, but Michael persevered, embracing the simplicity and freedom from calorie counting that the carnivore diet offered.

Within months, Michael's perseverance bore fruit. He experienced a significant weight loss and a newfound sense of vitality that breathed life into his everyday activities. As he delved into the combination of meat, fish, and eggs that became the cornerstones of his meals, he noticed a remarkable surge in his energy levels and mental clarity. Freed from the burden of counting calories and the draining efforts of traditional diets, Michael found a sense of liberation in the carnivore diet that spurred his journey forward.

Emboldened by his initial success, Michael began incorporating physical exercise into his routine. With newfound energy and mental clarity, he sought the guidance of a fitness trainer who tailored a workout plan that complemented his carnivore diet. Fuelled by the protein-rich meals and a renewed sense of vigor, Michael's transformation was nothing short of extraordinary. From being averse to physical activity, he transitioned into an enthusiastic athlete, participating in running events and embracing weight training with a zeal that he never thought possible.

Michael's journey serves as a shining example of the profound impact the carnivore diet can have on one's life. His transformation from a sedentary existence to an active and athletic lifestyle embodies the potential for renewal and revitalization that this dietary approach offers. Through his example, Michael provides hope and inspiration to individuals seeking a radical yet effective solution to their weight, health, and energy concerns. His story stands as a testimony to the transformative power of the carnivore diet for those willing to embark on the journey toward a healthier, more vibrant life.

Conclusion

As we reach the culmination of this transformative journey through the realm of the carnivore diet, I am filled with gratitude for the opportunity to guide you towards a path of rejuvenation and vitality. Through the exploration of the carnivore diet's principles, science, and practical applications, we have uncovered a paradigm shift in how we view nutrition, health, and holistic well-being. Together, we have delved into the depths of evolutionary heritage, the intricacies of nutrient-rich animal foods, and the profound impact of embracing a carnivorous lifestyle. As we bid farewell to these pages, I urge you to carry forward the torch of knowledge and empowerment that this book has ignited within you.

From the very genesis of this book, my intention has been to provide a beacon of hope for those who have felt disillusioned by the limitations of conventional diets. For the individuals grappling with weight issues, low energy levels, and a myriad of health concerns, the carnivore diet represents not just a dietary shift but a revolutionary reconnection with our ancestral roots. It offers a sanctuary of nourishment, a sanctuary of strength, and a sanctuary of simplicity in a world cluttered with conflicting nutritional advice.

Through the lens of personalized success stories like those of John's weight loss triumph, Sarah's autoimmune disease reversal, and Michael's journey from couch potato to athlete, we have witnessed the transformative potency of the carnivore diet. Each narrative serves as a testament to the resilience of the human body and the remarkable healing potential inherent in a diet focused on animal-based foods. These stories stand as monuments of inspiration for those seeking solace from the struggles of chronic health issues and unyielding weight challenges.

As we navigate the annals of chapters exploring the benefits, science, meal plans, and practical tips of the carnivore diet, I implore you to reflect on the simplicity and elegance of this approach to nutrition. Effortless weight loss, heightened energy levels, mental clarity, reduced inflammation, improved gut health, and hormone balance are not merely promises but tangible outcomes awaiting those who choose to embrace the carnivore lifestyle. The path to optimal health and holistic well-being is paved with the nutrient-dense bounty of animal products, offering a banquet of sustenance to fuel your journey forward.

In the cacophony of modern dietary dogmas and trends, the carnivore diet emerges as a bastion of authenticity and simplicity. It beckons you to shed the shackles of restrictive eating patterns and embrace a holistic approach that honors the innate wisdom of your body. By casting aside the misconceptions and fears surrounding red meat and animal fats, you open the door to a realm of gastronomic delights and nutritional abundance that can revitalize your existence from the inside out.

As we part ways, let the principles and teachings imparted within these chapters serve as guiding lights on your ongoing voyage towards health and vitality. Remember that the carnivore diet is not merely a temporary fix but a sustainable lifestyle choice that can recalibrate your relationship with food and reinvigorate your body, mind, and spirit. Embrace your inner carnivore with confidence and conviction, knowing that you hold the key to unlocking your true potential for optimal health and well-being.

Made in United States
Orlando, FL
27 November 2024

54558853R00061